Designed To Sell:
Turn-of-the-Century American Posters

in the Virginia Museum of Fine Arts

by Frederick R. Brandt
Curator, 20th-Century Art
Virginia Museum of Fine Arts

With essays by

Robert Koch

Philip B. Meggs

including a fully illustrated catalogue
of 111 posters in the collection of the
Virginia Museum of Fine Arts
compiled with the assistance of
M. Kathryn Shields

Virginia Museum of Fine Arts, Richmond

This book was originally published on the occasion of a special installation of posters from the collection of the Virginia Museum of Fine Arts, Richmond, November 9, 1994–January 8, 1995.

Tour Schedule

Selections from the Virginia Museum's American Posters Collection will also be shown in the following Museum Affiliate communities:

William King Regional Arts Center, Abingdon
March 11–May 15, 1995

Maier Museum of Art, Randolph-Macon Woman's College, Lynchburg, in collaboration with the Lynchburg Fine Arts Center
October 22–December 10, 1995

Peninsula Fine Arts Center, Newport News
November 12, 1996–January 7, 1997

Both this book and the special installation of posters in the Museum's galleries were made possible by funding from

The National Endowment for the Arts, Washington, D.C., a federal agency

and generous donations and gifts-in-kind from

The Collector Frame Shop, Richmond, Virginia

Sterling Printers, Inc., Richmond, Virginia

The Council of the Virginia Museum of Fine Arts

Life of Virginia

Universal Leaf Tobacco Company, Inc.

Nancy and Raymond Hunt

Library of Congress Cataloging-in-Publication Data
Brandt, Frederick R., 1936-
    Designed to sell: turn-of-the-century American posters in the Virginia Museum of Fine Arts / by Frederick R. Brandt; with essays by Robert Koch, Philip B. Meggs; including a fully illustrated catalogue of 111 posters in the collection of the Virginia Museum of Fine Arts compiled with the assistance of M. Kathryn Shields.
        p.   cm.
"Published on the occasion of a special installation of posters... November 9, 1994–January 8, 1995" —T.p. verso.
    Includes bibliographic references (p.   ) and index.
    ISBN 0-917046-38-2 (pbk.)
1. Posters, American—Exhibitions.   2. Posters—19th century—United States—Exhibitions.   3. Posters—20th century—United States—Exhibitions.   4. Advertising—United States—Posters—Exhibitions.   5. Posters—Virginia—Richmond—Exhibitions.   6. Virginia Museum of Fine Arts—Exhibitions.   I. Koch, Robert, 1918- .   II. Meggs, Philip B., 1942- .   III. Virginia Museum of Fine Arts.   IV. Title.
NC1849.A29B73   1994
741.6'74'0973074755451—dc20   94-32149
                                                                                                          CIP

ISBN 0-917046-38-2

Cover: *Read The Sun,* a poster designed by Louis Rhead to advertise the *New York Sun,* 1895 (cat. no. 93) is both a fine example of advertising art in its golden age and a symbol of the poster craze that swept America at the turn of the century. Beginning around 1895, American publishers began to commission the day's top artists and illustrators to help them promote an avalanche of new mass-market printed materials—newspapers, magazines, and pulp-fiction novels. Much to their surprise, the posters themselves were often as much in demand as the products they promoted. With this poster just off the presses, the artist promptly inscribed it for an avid collector.

Contents

Foreword

Although those of us in the museum world spend our lives surrounded by works of art, we seldom encounter an art form that has made its way so thoroughly into the everyday lives of so many others. Yet such a rare occurrence did happen with the bold and compelling posters, designed to sell, that pervaded the fabric of American life around the turn of the past century. These posters were at the leading edge of commerce and technology in their day, using all means possible to attract consumers to the latest products.

Now, hardly a hundred years later, we are in an era that fairly inundates us with words and images — to educate, entertain, and tantalize us with new products and services. Today, words and images are conveyed to us very differently from the communications of our ancestors. We might ask if this is done as dramatically or subtly, as whimsically or elegantly, as the posters set forth in this catalogue.

The Virginia Museum of Fine Arts is noted for its extensive collections of European and American Art Nouveau furniture, glass, and metalwork from the turn of the century. Yet few are aware that our collections include an especially fine array of vintage posters from a parallel period in American art.

Because these are works on paper, printed with impermanent inks, they are inherently fragile and can only rarely be placed on view. The special exhibition that prompted the publication of this catalogue allows our visitors the rare opportunity to see these beautiful and innovative works in person. The catalogue helps make this exceptional collection more widely known and accessible during times and circumstances when the posters themselves cannot be studied or savored in the original.

Katharine C. Lee
Director, Virginia Museum of Fine Arts

Preface & Acknowledgments

The exhibition that prompted this book is one of a series organized by the Virginia Museum of Fine Arts to show the strengths of various areas of its collections. As such, this is not only a book about a group of works from the permanent collection in a particular medium. It is also an attempt to show the deeper significance of these works—to their times, to their origins, and to the people who created them.

An exhibition of a significant collection of posters and the simultaneous publication of a comprehensive handbook such as this can only be accomplished through the combined efforts of many individuals. But before citing those involved in this project, acknowledgment must first be given to those who made the acquisition of the American poster collection possible for the Virginia Museum of Fine Arts.

Several posters were acquired in the early 1970s through the Sydney and Frances Lewis Art Nouveau Fund, with later additions made possible through purchases from the Adolph D. and Wilkins C. Williams Fund. The vast majority of these posters, however, were acquired in 1990 through the combined resources of the Museum's Arthur and Margaret Glasgow Fund and Sydney and Frances Lewis Endowment Fund. More recently, Dr. and Mrs. Robert Koch presented the Virginia Museum of Fine Arts with the generous gift of a large group of outstanding posters from this period. I wish to express my sincere gratitude to those who made these funds and gifts possible and thus made this collection, the present exhibition, and the accompanying publication a reality.

For the past two years, M. Kathryn Shields has worked diligently on this project, first as an intern and then as a Gallery Assistant. She has not only done extensive research into the collection but has also contributed to the catalogue of this collection by helping to compile the biographies of each of the artists involved in the creation of these dramatic images.

Dr. Robert Koch, Professor Emeritus of Southern Connecticut State University, has been an invaluable source of information in researching the exhibition and herein has contributed his scholarly essay on the artistic development of the American poster and its European antecedents. In addition to the poster gifts mentioned above, he and his wife, Gladys, also lent a number of "little magazines" to the museum for inclusion in the exhibition that was the occasion for this catalogue.

I wish to thank Philip B. Meggs, Professor of Communication Arts and Design at Virginia Commonwealth University, not only for his erudite essay and his insightful notes on the technical aspects of the American poster, but also for the many hours he spent carefully examining each poster in order to determine the specific graphic process used to produce it.

Another who has shared not only his knowledge but also part of his collection of "little magazines," books, and pamphlets to the exhibition is David R. Anderson. In addition, I want to thank the Alderman Library of the University of Virginia; Buffalo & Erie County Historical Society; Delaware Art Museum; Elbert Hubbard-Roycroft Museum, East Aurora, New York; Knight Capron Library, Lynchburg College, Lynchburg, Virginia; Richmond Public Library; and University Library, University of Texas at Arlington, for the loan of ancilliary objects to the exhibition including books, pamphlets, "little magazines," and preliminary artist's designs. It is through these materials that visitors to the exhibition will have a broader view of this short-lived but very intense period of graphic design in America, and can better understand the relationship of the posters to the products they were meant to promote.

Many members of the museum staff have been helpful and encouraging to me in bringing this exhibition and catalogue to fruition: Katharine C. Lee, Director, for her endorsement and support of the exhibition; Richard B. Woodward, Associate Director for Programs and Exhibitions, and Carol Moon, Assistant Manager for Exhibitions, for helping to guide the exhibition through its many phases; Diana Dougherty, Exective Secretary for Collections, for handling the countless details related to organizing both the exhibition and the catalogue; Lisa Hancock, Registrar, and her staff of Registrars and Art Handlers, for keeping track of the many details related to cataloging, framing, and installing the posters; Dan Brisbane, Preparator, for matting and framing the posters; Tom Baker, Exhibition Designer, for his innovative layout of the galleries; Deborah Frazier, Manager of Education and Outreach, and her staff, including Susan Glasser, Coordinator, Gallery Interpretation; Susan Ferrell, Coordinator, and Randee Humphrey, Assistant Coordinator, Affiliate Programs, for contributing to the educational aspects of the exhibition and for making it possible to circulate the exhibition to museum-affiliated organizations elsewhere in Virginia; Monica Rumsey, Editor-in-Chief, for her thoughtful editing of this book; Anne Barriault, Rosalie West, and Anne Lew, for their skillful copyediting and proofreading; Michelle Wilson and Christine Messing, for help in preparing the index; Jean Kane, Graphic Designer, for her clear and imaginative layout; Ron Jennings, Ann Hutchison, and Grace Wen Hwa Ts'ao, Museum Photographers, for their photodocumentation of the posters; Denise Lewis, for expert printing of the negatives for reproduction; Howell Perkins, for his dependable coordination of all aspects of photographic services; Margaret Burcham, Librarian, and Elizabeth Yevich, Library Cataloguer, for securing interlibrary loans for research; David B. Bradley, Associate Director, Development and Marketing, George T. Bryson, Jr., Assistant Director of Development, and Sharon Casale, Grants and Research Coordinator, for locating the funds necessary to make this project a reality; and to all others who have contributed in so many ways to this project.

I wish to thank The Council of the Virginia Museum of Fine Arts for its grant in support of this collection catalogue; John Cassell, whose company, the Collector Frame Shop, fabricated and donated the frames and mats for each of the posters as an in-kind contribution; the National Endowment for the Arts, a federal agency, for its funding; Sterling Printers, whose in-kind contribution made the printing of this book possible; Life of Virginia, for partial funding of the exhibition; Universal Leaf Tobacco Company, Inc., for their financial support of the exhibition poster; and Raymond and Nancy Hunt for their generous financial support.

Many colleagues in other institutions helped make this project a reality: Hydee Shaller, Director, The Mitchell Gallery, St. John's College, Annapolis, Maryland; Dr. William M.S. Rasmussen, Virginus C. Hall Curator of Art, Virginia Historical Society, Richmond; Betsy White, Director, William King Regional Arts Center, Abingdon, Virginia; Marie Via, Curatorial Assistant, Memorial Art Gallery, University of Rochester; and J. Alastair Duncan, Author and Curator, for their professional endorsements in support of this project.

Many other individuals have contributed in large and small ways to bring this exhibition about. These include Nancy Hunt, who began the original research that eventually developed into this catalogue; Ellie Bailey, of the Historical Society of Old Newbury, Newburyport, Massachusetts; Wendy Bellion, Library Assistant, the National Museum of Women in the Arts, Washington, D.C.; Casey Benney, Silvermine Guild Arts Center, New Canaan, Connecticut; Elizabeth Blakelock, Curatorial Assistant, the Connecticut Historical Society; Bruce Bland, Co-Curator, Elbert Hubbard-Roycroft Museum, East Aurora, New York; Charles E. Brown, Manager, Information Services, Merc Source, Mercantile Library, St. Louis, Missouri; The Connecticut State Department of Health Services; Mr. Robert N. Costa, Director, Richmond Public Library; Mrs. B. Warwick Davenport, Richmond, Virginia; Lee Ann Dean, Archivist, Helen Farr Sloan Library, and Dr. Mary Holahan, Registrar, Delaware Art Museum, Wilmington; Kari E. Horowicz, Librarian, Albright-Knox Art Gallery, Buffalo, New York; Douglas P. Hurd, Interlibrary Services/Loans, Alderman Library, University of Virginia, Charlottesville; Bridget Knightly, Library Assistant, The Bostonian Society; Emily Miller, Public Services Librarian, Missouri Historical Society, St. Louis; Debra Armstrong-Morgan, Registrar, Humanities Research Center, University of Austin, Texas; Richard W. Oram, Librarian, Harry Ransom Humanities Research Center, The University of Texas at Austin; Walt Reed, Illustration House, Inc., New York, New York; Mrs. Joan G. Robidoux, Norwalk Historical Commission; the Staff of the Earl Gregg Swem Library, College of William and Mary, Williamsburg, Virginia; Eleanor McD. Thompson, Librarian in Charge, Printed Book & Periodical Collection, The Winterthur Library, Wilmington, Delaware; George Theofiles, of Miscellaneous Man in New Freedom, Pennsylvania; Jean-François Vilain, Senior Editor, F. A. Davis Company, Philadelphia; and Lee Viverette, Archives of American Art, Smithsonian Institution, Washington, D.C.

Finally, I want to express my gratitude to Sydney and Frances Lewis, whose countless gifts of extraordinary late nineteenth- and early twentieth-century decorative arts gave me the inspiration to mount this exhibition, and for their generous endowment, which made the purchase of many of these posters possible.

—FRB

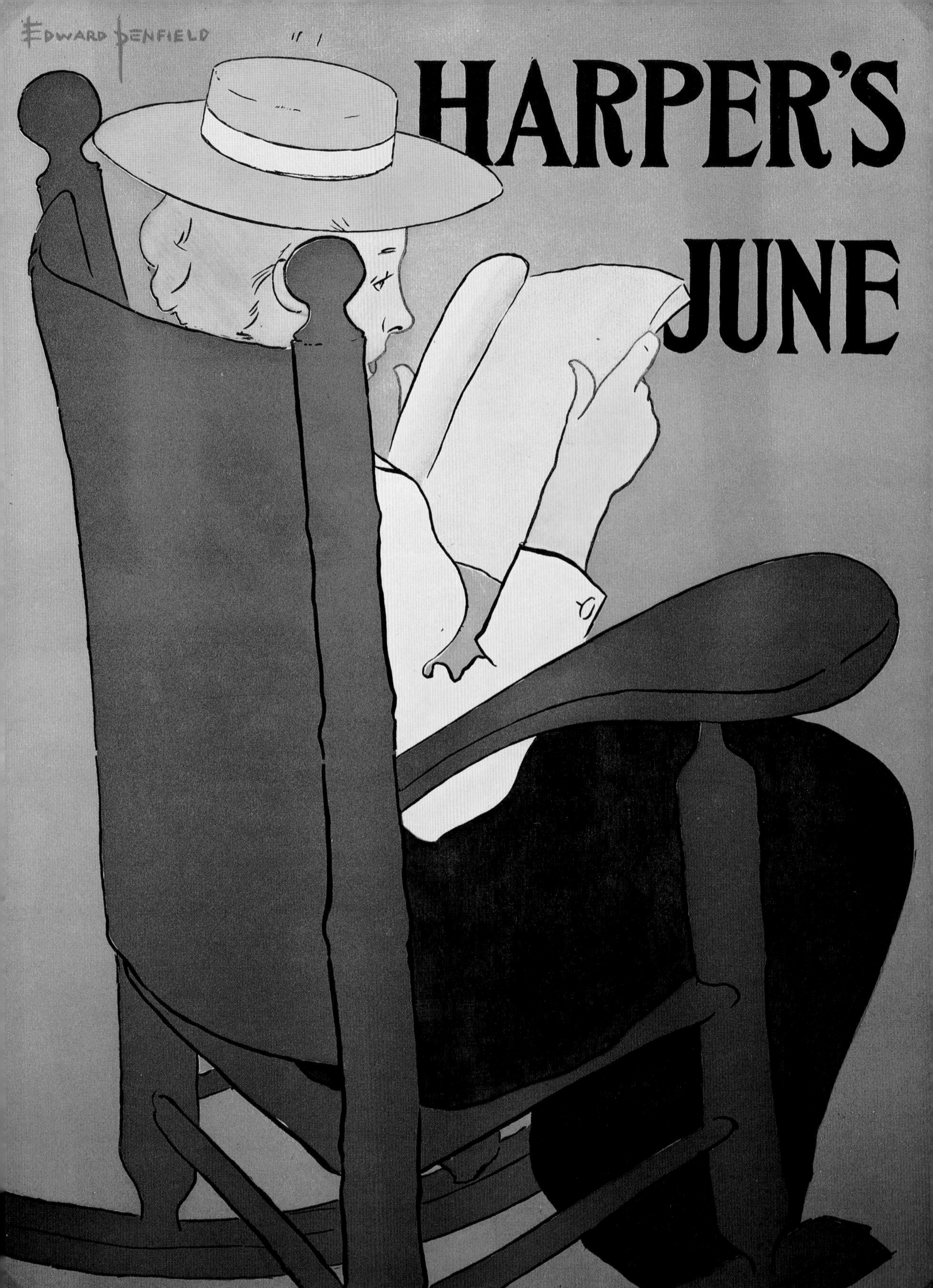
EDWARD PENFIELD
HARPER'S
JUNE

CHAPTER 1

Introduction:
Posters, Patrons, and Publishers

by Frederick R. Brandt

"In America—at least, in the United States—the poster enjoys an absolutely unique distinction. In other countries, it has been prized and admired, cherished in costly collections, and honored with the most serious artistic study and criticism. But in the United States the poster has been—and in some parts of the land it is yet— not only admired but loved."

H. C. Bunner, 1895[1]

Posters: The Spirit of a New Century

Evidently posters were loved in America during the last decade of the 1800s, if one can judge admiration of such an art form by the number that were produced and collected during what has been termed the golden age of American posters, from about 1894 to 1905. In his essay, published as Chapter 2 of this catalogue, American poster expert Dr. Robert Koch has traced the development of the poster in the United States in relation to those produced in England and France. It is important to realize, however, that the incredible development of the American poster in such a short period of time, as well as the accompanying passion for collecting posters, came about due to a series of conditions involving increased literacy, publication for the masses, and new advances in print technology that all witnessed dramatic growth and development in this country at that time.

With urban expansion and improved standards of living, just before and after the turn of the last century, Americans became better educated, and their improved financial conditions permitted them to have more time to read as a leisure pastime (**figure 1.1**) or to pursue outdoor recreation (**figure 1.2**). As a result, literary circles and book clubs were founded, and popular novels and so-called little magazines were more frequently published.

The cultural historian Frank Luther Mott has indicated that a major cause of the increase in less expensive magazines was due to "the directed and organized passion for self-improvement, the mass move-

Figure 1.1. Edward Penfield's posters for *Harper's* magazine often depicted members of the middle or upper classes reading as a leisure-time activity. Penfield's work was praised by his colleague, a pioneer of American poster design, Will H. Bradley.

Edward Penfield
Harper's June, 1896 (cat. no. 66)

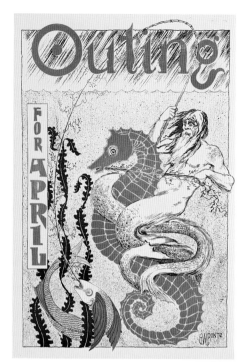

Figure 1.2. As Americans became better educated around the turn of the century, improved financial circumstances allowed them more time to read and relax. Special magazines, such as *Outing*, were published to appeal to readers' interests, in this case with ingenuity, humor, and flair.

George Willard Bonte
Outing for April, 1897 (cat. no. 7)

ment toward adult education [amongst the middle class]."[2] Mott has also pointed out the decline in price of the popular magazine from the usual, previous, and more expensive thirty-five cents, aimed at the aristocratic and moneyed class, to the ten-cent magazine geared more toward the man on the street.

At the same time, magazine publishers saw the need to take on social causes and reforms as their primary editorial thrust, and to publish materials designed to serve the interests of a constantly growing younger audience. Besides promoting literature that had social reform as its purpose, many artists and publishers felt that the arts and crafts could be made to serve the general populace, regardless of social background or financial status, and should be widely available.

The mid-nineteenth-century English reformer/artists, such as John Ruskin and William Morris, stood for an idealistic philosophy that would do away with social and environmental inequities and raise the standard of living, if not to the elevated status of the upper class, at least to a comfortable standard that would ensure health and well-being. These idealists felt that art had the potential for strong curative powers. This same philosophy was carried forth by some of America's most prominent poster artists, such as the English-born Louis Rhead, who firmly believed that the poster, as the poor-man's art gallery, could enrich everyday life. Rhead often referred to the "moral aspect of the artistic poster."[3]

All of these factors—demographic, philosophic, and aesthetic—combined with the growth of national advertising and marketing, as well as new developments in technology such as photo-mechanical halftone printing **(figure 1.3)**—resulted in an unparalleled increase in the printing of magazines and popular novels. As a result, the advertising and promotion of these printed materials increased in the form of the ubiquitous poster, which served not only to promote visually these new mass-market publications, but also to enrich the owner's life and home.

By 1896 author Will M. Clemens had already noted that, due to the public demand for posters, "In the United States there are today something like twenty establishments which make posters alone their special production, and which show a capital invested of nearly $3,000,000. They provide employment for something like one hundred draughtsmen and designers, and perhaps five hundred additional artists who reproduce the originals of the former. . . . All progressive art stores have poster displays."[4]

In relation to this surge of poster production, the critic Roger Cunningham commented, "And quickly we hear the very hawking cry of commerce made musical, and we see the hoarding become an art gallery, for the art which was fresh, the unfinished sketch, which contained a soul—the artist had only been able to finish its body for exhibition within a gold frame prison—the *free,* bold symbolism of thought, which could find no place in the 'Monthly Ambler' of that past, came forth, reveling in unchained liberty of line and form and color, and artist souls were glad."[5]

Figure 1.3. With increased competition among publishers, posters were commissioned to help attract the customer's eye at the bookstand.

Henry Sumner Watson
July 1895 Outing (cat. no. 106)

Figure 1.4. In the early days of poster design, artists found it necessary to defend the legitimacy of their art against snobbish detractors, who considered their work "decadent" and "diabolically modern." One artist, Claude Fayette Bragdon, defended American poster design with eloquence and insight.

Claude Fayette Bragdon
The Chap-Book, 1895 (cat. no. 22)

More recently, the poster of a century ago has also been looked upon admirably: "The poster possessed a sophistication and universal appeal that united at its best High Art and Low Life. The boldness of the new discipline, an art form in its own right, was to become a major formative influence on the arts of the 20th century."[6]

In the early days of the American poster, not everyone agreed with H. C. Bunner's assessment that posters were "not only admired, but loved" in this country. Some felt that the art of the poster was decadent and that posters were "fantastic, disjointed, perverse, bedaubed, uniquely new, and diabolically modern."[7] Why someone would consider something "uniquely new" to be reprehensible or diabolical is not easily understood. Perhaps such writers considered the art of the poster "decadent" because of the association of the graphic medium with the notoriety of such English aesthetes as Aubrey Beardsley and Oscar Wilde.

Others, including the artists themselves, rushed to the defense of their chosen art form **(figure 1.4)**. In 1896 Claude Fayette Bragdon wrote: "The People who still scoff at posters and poster collecting should bear in mind that the great periods of art were those in which it allied itself most intimately with the daily life of the people, and that in this craze for posters, 'the poor man's picture gallery,' as they are called, is seen almost the first sign of a renaissance in which the spirit of the century, which is so largely a commercial one, will find an utterance in beauty instead of ugliness."[8]

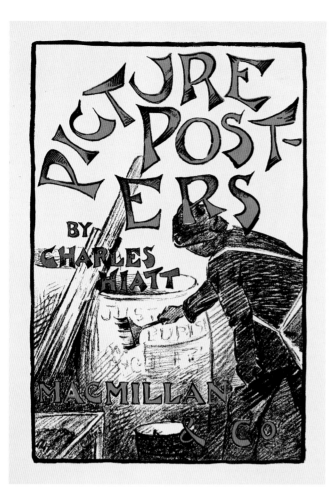

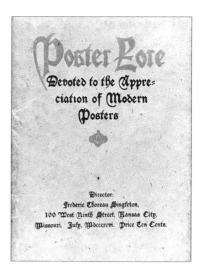

Figure 1.6. Such periodicals as *Poster Lore*—out of Kansas City, Missouri, in the mid 1890s—are evidence of the spread of the poster craze by the end of the nineteenth century. In fact Frederic Singleton, publisher of this magazine, flatly acknowledged that many posters were more popular than the publications they were designed to sell.

Cover, *Poster Lore*, (July 1896), Collection of Dr. and Mrs. Robert Koch.

Figure 1.5. As early as 1893, English art critic Charles Hiatt was writing about poster aesthetics and connoisseurship. This lively poster promoted one of his books.

Artist Unknown
Picture Posters by Charles Hiatt,
1895 (cat. no. 3)

In spite of the acclamations in favor of American posters and their collecting, certain chroniclers of American art of that time still placed the American poster in a very minor and secondary role: "The artistic poster had only a short reign in America," observed art historian S. Hartmann in 1902. "It started about 1895 and subsided within the year. The only truly artistic work that was done was a poster for the New York *Sun* [he was probably referring to a poster by Louis Rhead], and a theatrical poster for the 'Masqueraders,' by Will H. Bradley, and some smaller designs by Ethel Reed and E. Penfield."[9] From such a close vantage-point, it is not surprising that Hartmann failed to consider the entire span and impact of the poster craze. Perhaps he felt that lack of artistic merit had been the cause of the short life of this fad. In fact, the artists whose work he cited are rarely considered significant in today's surveys of graphic arts history. Among Hartmann's examples were posters by Peter Newell, Walter Appleton Clar, Eric Pape, A. T. Keller, and many others whose works have become obscured behind the veil of time and greater historical perspective.

Another subject of great debate in the heyday of the American poster were the very words used to describe the artist who created posters. Will Bradley, writing about his colleague Edward Penfield, said: "One might say 'poster' artist, for it is through his posters that we have come to know him; yet such a title leaves an unpleasant impression on the mind, and one prefers to speak of him simply as Edward Penfield, Artist"[10] **(figure 1.1)**.

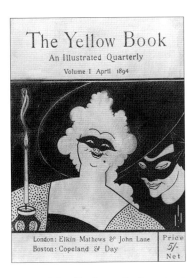

Figure 1.7. The innovative layout and provocative content of this imported British magazine made it an instant success among American readers, and helped promote the craze for so-called "little magazines."

Aubrey Beardsley
Cover, *The Yellow Book,* vol. 1, no. 1 (April 1894), Collection of Frederick and Carol Brandt.

Again, it was poster critic Roger Cunningham who raised the specter of the title "poster artist" when he wrote: "But why 'poster artists'? An artist, if artist he be at all, is simply artist, pure and unqualified. The word admits of no agnomen. He who is artist when making a poster is artist othertimes and all the time."[11]

The English art critic Charles Hiatt, who wrote extensively about posters **(figure 1.5)**, commented as early as 1893 on the quality of posters in relation to the country in which they were designed. Hiatt felt that the collecting of posters was a new field for connoisseurs but cautioned collectors that the best posters were those produced in France, while the poster in his native England "rarely succeeds in being other than abominable. . . . [and] it is only fair to say that in the States they have escaped the ugliness and stupidity which are still rampant in England."[12] Comparatively speaking, Hiatt even commented that the American designers "turn out pretty things enough. . . . "[13]

The artist Claude Fayette Bragdon commented on the "absence of the element of humor in these [American] productions of the most humor-loving nation in the world. Whatever be their other excellencies—and they are many— our posters surely fail both in the irrepressible joyousness, and in the quiet humor of many of the foreign posters."[14] To support his criticism, he cited examples by Bradley, Penfield, and Rhead.

In addition, Bragdon encouraged the creation of strong visual images in America by urging young poster designers to try to put a good idea into "some simple, pleasing and readily intelligible form. Work it out first on a small scale, roughly, and in monochrome, vigorously suppressing detail, which is the enemy of design. Then increase the size of your drawing and elaborate it further. . . . "[15]

Many writers of the period discussed the cost of posters. Frederic Thoreau Singleton, the Director [editor and publisher] of the magazine *Poster Lore* **(figure 1.6)** felt that "twenty-five cents is a good price to pay for an art poster with lettering. It is un-American anyhow, for publishers to charge for their advertising matter. They do these better in London and on the Continent, where one has to pay even for a price-list. Because I have to pay for my posters I cannot buy so many books. I purchase the poster now when once I would purchase the book, and I do not think my publishers profit thereby. As for my profit—well, I prefer the poster."[16]

It is this very attitude toward collecting posters versus buying books that ultimately led to the demise of the art poster in the early twentieth century. Eventually, publishers put more of their resources behind the printing and publication of their books and magazines and less into advertising them through the poster.

Poster Patrons and Collectors

The short-lived but overwhelming flood of posters and "little magazines" of this period can be traced back to 1894, with the introduction to America of John Lane's *The Yellow Book* **(figure 1.7)**, featuring graphics by Aubrey Beardsley. The journal's innovative layout, controversial literary content, and imaginative design and graphics immedi-

ately appealed to the American public as it had in Europe although, in both cases, it caused much concern for its unconventional content.

Just prior to that, Edward Penfield, as art editor for *Harper's*, produced his first poster in the new style for that magazine, and the first issue of *The Chap-Book* appeared with a poster design by Will H. Bradley. According to art historian Diane Chalmers Johnson, this small periodical *(The Chap-Book)* "seems to have started the American 'craze' for collecting posters, and before long its advertising pages carried a standing price list of its own posters. . . . Thus the two 'crazes' of the 1890's, periodical and posters, developed together."[17]

An interesting compilation, description, and survey of the "little magazines" and their phenomenal rise was published as *Ephemeral Bibelots* by Frederick Winthorp Faxon in 1903. In this he comments: "The small, artistically printed periodicals variously called Chapbooks, Ephemerals, Bibelots, Brownie Magazines, Fadazines, Magazettes, Freak Magazines, owe their origin probably to the success of the *Chap-Book*, a little semi-monthly magazine which was born in Cambridge on May 15, 1894, and which was at once in such great demand that all the early numbers were soon out of print. . . . "[18]

Faxon then comments on the rise of what he cites as its imitators, and lists 229 "Ephemeral Bibelots" with their date, frequency, and place of publication, ranging from *The Alkahest* to *The Yellow Kid*.[19]

Publishers sponsored poster-design competitions to attract the most talented artists to their magazines. In 1896, *The Century* sponsored such a contest and Maxfield Parrish won second prize with his sensitive design of a nude sitting pensively before a wooded landscape (**figure 1.8**). It is said that Parrish only received second prize because his design would have required four colors to print while only three were permitted for the contest.[20]

Other major publishers followed suit with designs by many known and relatively unknown graphic artists such as Will Carqueville, Frank Hazenplug, J. C. Leyendecker (**figure 1.9**), Blanche McManus (**figure 1.10**), Ethel Reed, John Sloan, and others. These artists created posters as advertisements for such major publishing houses as J. B. Lippincott Co., Charles Scribner's Sons (**figure 1.11**), Harper's, and The Century Co. Some posters were created specifically for collectors.

Although produced to advertise the *New York Sun*, the poster *Read the Sun* (**figure 1.12**) by Louis J. Rhead in the Virginia Museum's collection is inscribed in ink: "To Wilbur M. [Macy] Stone Hartford Conn. with regards Louis J. Rhead. This copy and one I am sending to Bolton [Charles Knowles Bolton, then the foremost poster collector in the country] are the 2 first allowed to leave the 'Sun' office." This statement makes it clear how sought-after new issues of posters were among the leading collectors and friends of the artists. The inscription further demonstrates that sometimes the collectors got the posters just as they came off of the press, even before they were publicly distributed.

Figure 1.8. A gifted young artist by the name of Maxfield Parrish only won second prize for his poster in the 1896 competition sponsored by *Century* magazine. He apparently missed first place only because his design required printing in four colors, and the contest rules set the limit at three inks.

Maxfield Parrish
The Century Midsummer Holiday Number, August, 1897 (cat. no. 62)

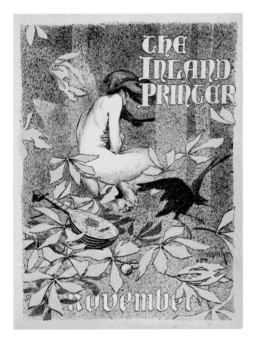

Figure 1.9. Like J. C. Leyendecker, many successful illustrators of the early twentieth century began their careers designing posters for commercial and trade publishers.

Joseph Christian Leyendecker
The Inland Printer, November 1896
(cat. no. 48)

Figure 1.10. A surprising number of women were among the most talented illustrators and poster designers during the "golden age" of poster design.

Blanche McManus
The True Mother Goose, 1895
(cat. no. 55)

Figure 1.11. Even the most successful publishers, such as Charles Scribner's Sons, understood that strong advertising images could ensure them an edge over the competition.

Will H. Low
Scribner's Fiction Number, 1895
(cat. no. 52)

Figure 1.12. Truly a "collectors' edition" poster: fresh off the presses, this poster was promptly inscribed by the artist, in his own hand, to a friend and avid poster collector (see inscription, lower right).

Louis John Rhead
Read the Sun, 1895
(cover and cat. no. 93)

Figure 1.13. The popularity of posters as early "collectibles" was enhanced by limited-edition books and accompanying posters, such as this one.

Will H. Bradley
The Modern Poster, 1895 (cat. no. 18)

Figure 1.14. Besides helping to sell books and magazines, many posters were commissioned to promote other new products, such as household goods, foods, patent medicines, and bicycles.

R. J. Campbell
Victor Cycles, 1898 (cat. no. 24)

Before long, poster "parties" and so-called living poster shows [21] were held, while small journals devoted exclusively to poster collecting were also being published. Books on posters were also produced, such as *The Modern Poster* (1895), in an edition limited to a thousand, each with an accompanying poster **(figure 1.13)** by Bradley. In an 1896 issue of *The Poster,* publisher Will M. Clemens noted, "There are upwards of six thousand poster collectors in the United States, and fully a thousand in Canada."[22] It was also estimated that at this time some collections already included more than a thousand posters.

Posters were originally sent to the newsstands to advertise the publication of a new issue of a journal, periodical, or book. Soon, however, they were being sold at the newsstands when it was found that the posters themselves had become more popular than the products they advertised. Eventually, companies realized that the posters conflicted with the production and sale of their products and the poster production and "craze" came to a halt. As Joseph Goddu recently wrote in a catalogue accompanying a poster exhibition at the New York galleries of Hirschl & Adler, "For a brief, yet glorious period nearly a century ago [the aesthetic and philosophical] aspirations were realized, in works whose legacy provides a rich addition to the history of American art."[23]

At the turn of the century, posters had served as advertisements for a wide variety of products: bicycles, then a relatively new product **(figure 1.14)**; food and wine; cafés and restaurants; cabaret and circus

Figure 1.16. Some of the most successful graphic artists later published their own journals and advertising posters.

Will H. Bradley
Cover, *Bradley, His Book,* 1896,
Collection of Dr. and Mrs. Robert Koch.

Figure 1.15. Toward the end of the nineteenth century, the proliferation of cultural events and a growing desire for personal enrichment led to the publication of books and promotional posters designed to make the fine arts more accessible to the general public.

Irene Weir
Opera Stories, 1896 (cat. no 108)

performers; and especially the small popular journals that suddenly seemed to appear everywhere.

Elbert Hubbard, founder of The Roycrofters, an arts and crafts community in East Aurora, New York, sarcastically commented on the upsurge of little magazines and journals in 1895: "We now have the *Lotus*, the *Lotos*, and the *Lettuce*. The latest is the *Prairie Dog*. Its hole is in Lawrence, Kansas, and it is patterned after the *Chip-Monk*. Verily, like begets like."[24]

Although Hubbard undoubtedly made this statement somewhat tongue-in-cheek, he himself contributed a number of magazines to the several hundred that were eventually produced.

The editors of *The Chap-Book* took note of Hubbard's comments and responded to it in their July 1, 1895 issue: "It is one of the evidences of all great art, to arouse imitation. . . . the sincerest form of flattery comes to me from East Aurora, New York, rejoicing in the happy name *The Philistine*. . . . a certain Mr. Elbert Hubbard . . . was now indulging in the pastime of driving periodicals tandem. . . . *The Chap-Book* figuring as *"The Chip-Munk"* seems to bulk very large in the Philistinic field of vision, and the doughty Elbert and his pals use most of their space thrusting at it."[25] This lighthearted bantering between periodical editors seems to have continued during their short-lived runs as they vied for top position in popularity and sales.

Many of the little magazines were printed on flimsy paper without much thought to endurance or longevity, while others had elaborate color covers and were printed on slick stock. To further complete the circle, many of the new magazines and journals included listings of posters that one could purchase as individual items.

This proliferation of magazines and journals was no doubt closely connected with the rising literacy rate in America at the time, and the overwhelming public desire for "culture" (**figure 1.15**). Many of these publications contained works by unknown and soon-forgotten authors; others introduced authors who eventually became recognized masters of their craft. Some illustrators, such as Will H. Bradley, even published their own periodicals. In Bradley's case it was *Bradley, His Book*, issued during 1896–97 (**figure 1.16**).

Posters by Women

Although a great majority of turn-of-the-century American posters depicted female subjects, most of the poster artists recognized during their lifetime, and even until today, were male. The field of poster design was perceived as being dominated by what one author referred to as "a young man's style: bold, simple and of unorthodox composition,"[26] yet a great number of very talented women artists contributed immeasurably to the art of the American poster. Until recently, much of their work has been ignored in favor of their better-known male counterparts.

In an unbelievably sexist essay about the artist Ethel Reed published in *The Poster* in November, 1898, S. C. De Soissons noted, "One can understand that women have no originality of thought, and that literature and music have no feminine character, but surely

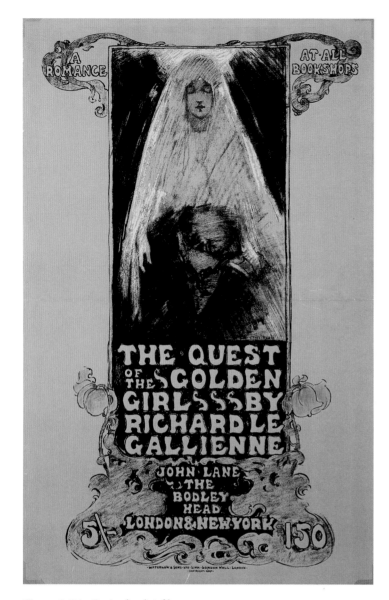

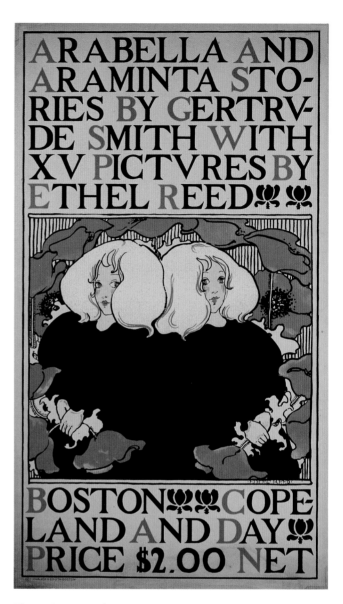

Figure 1.17. During her brief but productive career, American artist Ethel Reed created some of the most compelling poster designs and book illustrations of her era. This was her last known design.

Ethel Reed
Quest of the Golden Girl, 1898
(cat. no. 91)

Figure 1.18. Reed's engaging poster featuring two precocious young ladies apparently inspired the nickname for romantic fiction of the day—"yellow-hair library."

Ethel Reed
Arabella and Araminta Stories,
1895 (cat. no. 82)

women know how to observe, and what they see is quite different from that which men see, and the art which they put in their gestures, in their dresses, in the decoration of their environment, is sufficient to give us the idea of an instinctive and peculiar genius which each of them possesses.

"Strictly speaking, woman only has the right to practice the system of the impressionist; she herself can limit her efforts and translate her impressions and recompense the superficial by her incomparable charm, her fine grace, and her sweetness."[27]

The use of such chauvinistic terms to describe a preeminent artist and book illustrator of the late nineteenth century is almost incomprehensible to us today. During her brief career, Ethel Reed produced some of the most dynamic and graphically beautiful posters and book illustrations of the period.

Ethel Reed is an enigma, however, having reached a pinnacle of success in America by 1896 and then virtually disappearing. Although highly regarded as an artist and engaged to marry the Boston painter Philip Hale, she was reported to be taking a vacation alone in London and working on her last known poster, *Quest of the Golden Girl,* published in 1898 **(figure 1.17)**. Later she was said to be resting in Ireland,[28] but nothing further is known of her after 1900.

During this very brief period of production, Reed created a style that is immediately recognizable, and she became one of the most popular image-makers of the period. Like other artists of the day, she was obviously influenced by Japanese art. This is evident in her use of flat, unshaded areas of color and silhouettes of figures in her posters and book illustrations.

In most of her posters, Reed featured images of one or several similar precocious young girls, possibly based on self-portraits. They are surrounded by flowers and appear to be imbued with an intriguing combination of innocence and turn-of-the-century seductive symbolism, reminiscent of a collection of poems, *Les Fleurs du mal* by Charles Baudelaire, and its relationship to decadent themes in the late nineteenth-century Symbolist and Art Nouveau movements. Reed's poster for *Arabella and Araminata Stories* **(figure 1.18)** of 1895, depicting golden-haired twins, is said to have given the popular series of romantic fiction its name, "The Yellow Hair Library."[29]

Florence Lundborg, another successful female artist, was a designer and painter from the West Coast of the United States. She is perhaps best known for her contributions to the short-lived small magazine *The Lark*, published by William Doxey and edited by Gelett Burgess. For just two years, this charming, witty, and irreverent magazine published the writings of Burgess, Jack London, Frank Norris, Arnold Genthe, Upton Sinclair, and others, who formed a unique group reflecting the aesthetics of the California style.

Lundborg not only produced posters for *The Lark*, but also illustrations for many of the covers and articles published in the periodical. Feeling that woodblock designs had "more of the personality of their inventor than the mechanically produced lithograph [could] possibly have," she insisted on cutting the blocks for the woodcuts herself.[30]

Figure 1.19. With hand-cut lettering and a woodcut image printed on Chinese bamboo paper, this poster shows that the California Arts and Crafts Movement was sensitive to the influence of the arts of Asia at the turn of the century.

Florence Lundborg
The Lark, "What is That Mother?"
August 1895 (cat. no. 53)

Figure 1.20. In the male-dominated world of a century ago, talented women artists had few opportunities to achieve public recognition for their work. Evelyn Rumsey Cary did find acclaim when her oil painting of the mythical Niagara was adapted as the poster icon for the Pan-American Exposition, 1901.

Evelyn Rumsey Cary
Pan-American Exposition, Buffalo,
1901 (cat. no. 29)

However, for the 1895 poster in the Virginia Museum collection (**figure 1.19**), Lundborg entrusted the cutting of the block to artist/editor Gelett Burgess. The block was then printed on "a very interesting Bamboo fibre paper used [as wrapping paper] in the Chinese drug stores in San Francisco."[31] The relative simplicity of the woodcut, the woman's medieval style of dress, and the artist's hand-lettering in this poster all combine to form an interesting example of the West Coast Arts and Crafts Movement at the turn of the century.

Evelyn Rumsey Cary (**figure 1.20**), Blanche McManus, Violet Oakley, and Irene Weir are but a few of the other talented women artists who brought their unique visions to this very public form of art but whose work has thus far been overshadowed by their male contemporaries.

New Technology for a New Age

The magazine is neither unique to America nor to its initial rise as a form of publishing at the turn of the century: it had existed in one form or another for many years in the United States. One could even consider Ben Franklin's *Poor Richard's Almanac* an eighteenth-century prototype of the "little magazine." As has already been noted, however, the reduction of price and consequently wider availability to the general public prompted the great proliferation of magazines and the popularity of the poster.

It is interesting to consider that some similarities exist between the rapid rise of the small-format magazines and their companion posters, aimed at the middle-class in the late 1800s, and the equally spectacular rise of commercial television broadcasting just fifty years later, in the late 1940s and early 1950s. As early as the 1920s, inventors had been experimenting and tinkering with mechanical television, finally producing marketable sets just before World War II.

New technology contributed to the proliferation of magazines, posters, and television—through advances in printing techniques in one case and electronic circuitry in the other. Both were, and for the most part television still is, originally aimed at the middle class, in their verbal and visual content. One is almost tempted to draw further comparison between the "intellectual" little magazines, such as *The Lark*, and the "highbrow" television programs produced today for public educational stations, while the popular novels and short stories of the past century have more than a close resemblance to the sit-coms and soap operas of today's commercial network programming.

Except for specially subsidized programs, television sponsorship is dominated by popular products not unlike those advertised in the turn-of-the-century posters and magazines. In any of these journals one can readily find advertisements for patent medicines, furniture sales, ways to improve one's moral and physical character, soap and other cleaning products, etc. Parallel advertisements in posters, magazines, and television and their accompanying hyperbole flood the market with the hope of luring the reader or the viewer to buy the product. Both television advertisements and the early magazines and posters were considered to be ephemeral, constantly changing as social standards and status of living changed.

Figure 1.21A. The directness of this composition owes a debt to the teachings of Arthur Wesley Dow, whose poster images blended line, mass, and color with stark simplicity.

Georgia O'Keeffe
Light Iris, 1924, oil on canvas; collection of the Virginia Museum of Fine Arts, Gift of Mr. and Mrs. Bruce C. Gottwald, accession no. 85.1534.

Figure 1.21. Strength through simplicity and compatibility between type and image have always been the measure of great poster design.

Arthur Wesley Dow
Modern Art, 1895 (cat. no. 33)

Like printed matter before better print technology lowered costs, the first television sets of the early 1950s were also beyond the means of the average American household. But as technology grew and industry competed to produce less expensive models, the television set, too, became a standard item rather than a luxury. Like television, the early magazines and their posters have shaped our everyday lives, our culture, our mores, and our politics. Leisure time that had once been consumed by reading "dime-store novels" and "little magazines" was now taken up by watching television. The only notable difference between these two mass-media products is that posters for magazines and books have been replaced by magazine and newspaper advertisements for television programs.

Posters as Mirrors of Other Arts

Museums have long acknowledged that the poster is a legitimate art form and, like private collectors, have acquired them. Known internationally for its collections of Art Nouveau, Arts and Crafts, and Art Déco design and decorative arts, the Virginia Museum of Fine Arts has also collected posters of the same period. Relationships can be drawn between many of these American posters and works in other areas of the permanent collection. For example, the teachings of Arthur Wesley Dow—combining line, mass, and color to add structure to the image, and using a careful building process to create beauty through simplicity **(figure 1.21)**—can be seen in the painting *Light Iris* by Dow's student, Georgia O'Keeffe **(figure 1.21A)**.

Figure 1.22A. Harvey Ellis, ***Fall-Front Desk,*** 1903-04, quarter-sawn white oak with poplar and other woods, with pewter and copper, designed for Gustav Stickley's Craftsman Workshops and distributed by Cobb-Eastman Co., Boston, Massachusetts. Collection of the Virginia Museum of Fine Arts, Gift of Sydney and Frances Lewis, accession no. 85.70.

Figure 1.22. Architect/designer Harvey Ellis, who was fluent in both two- and three-dimensional design, knew that balance and proportion are as essential to poster design as they are to furniture and architecture.

Harvey Ellis
Harper's Christmas, 1898 (cat. no. 36)

The architect/designer Harvey Ellis worked for the leading Arts and Crafts proponent Gustav Stickley for only one year, but in that time Ellis brought unique concepts to Stickley's design idiom. Ellis's posters **(figure 1.22)** bring the same Arts and Crafts ideas to the printed media that he eventually imbued in his three-dimensional designs for furniture **(figure 1.22A)** and buildings.

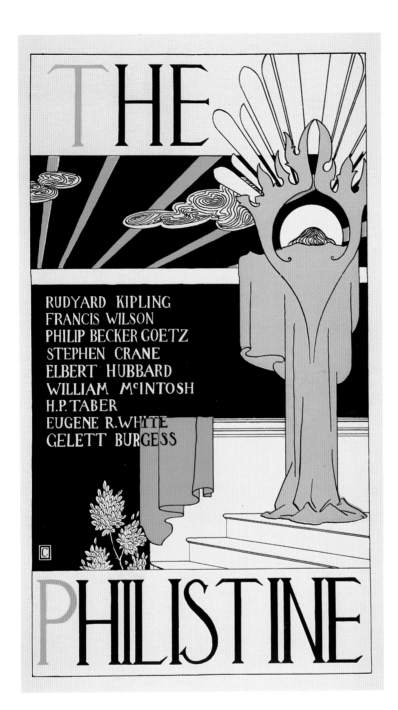

Figure 1.23A. Bringing the Roycroft aesthetic home: Roycroft furniture followed the Hubbard ideal of practical beauty punctuated by simple adornment.

Magazine Pedestal, 1902, from the Roycroft Shops, East Aurora, New York. Collection of the Virginia Museum of Fine Arts, Purchase, The Mary Morton Parsons Fund for American Decorative Arts, accession no. 78.128.

Figure 1.23. Elbert Hubbard established his Arts and Crafts community and studio, The Roycrofters, in East Aurora, outside Buffalo, New York, in 1895. His literary journal, *The Philistine*, carried out new ideas about art and culture, and strong poster designs would carry the message to newsstand browsers.

Dwight Ripley Collin
The Philistine, July 1895 (cat. no. 30)

Similarly, Elbert Hubbard established The Roycrofters, a dynamic craft-making community in East Aurora, New York, to produce Arts and Crafts books, magazines, metalwork, leather goods, and furniture **(figure 1.23A)**. Hubbard commissioned the talented Dwight Ripley Collin to design a somewhat enigmatic poster for his literary magazine, *The Philistine* **(figure 1.23)**.[32] And finally, William Sargeant Kendall's 1895

Figure 1.24A. The Virginia Museum's collection includes a painting by the artist featured in the Sergeant Kendall poster.

Robert Blum, **Temple Court of Fudo Sama at Meguro, Tokyo,** 1891, oil on canvas, Collection of the Virginia Museum of Fine Arts, Purchase, The J. Harwood and Louise B. Cochrane Fund for American Art, accession no. 91.503.

Figure 1.24. William Sargeant Kendall, who created this poster for *Scribner's,* apparently had a clear grasp of the visual power of blank space and asymmetry. The spare, hand-drawn lettering and informal subject represent a bold break with turn-of-the-century aesthetics.

William Sargeant Kendall
Robert Blum's Great Decorative Painting in January Scribner's, 1895 (cat. no. 46)

poster for *Robert Blum's Great Decorative Painting* is considered one of the most elegant posters of this period **(figure 1.24)**. Four years earlier, Blum had painted the *Temple Court Fudo Sama at Meguro, Tokyo,* now in the Virginia Museum's collection **(figure 1.24A)**.

Many stylistic comparisons can be drawn between objects in the museum's Art Nouveau collection and posters, like Will Bradley's for *The Chap-Book* of 1894 **(figure 1.25)**, judged by Dr. Robert Koch to be the first American Art Nouveau poster.

This book attempts to show how art not only imitates life but also has a life of its own. In the history of poster-making in America, what began as unpretentious printed ephemera has now become widely recognized both as a document of America's social and cultural history, and as a significant art form in its own right. ◻

Figure 1.25. The blossoming of American poster design out of European prototypes can be seen in this dynamic American poster. Here, the creativity of the young Will Bradley takes up where his stylistic mentor, the English artist and illustrator Aubrey Beardsley, left off (compare figure 3.8, p.42).

Will H. Bradley
The Chap-Book, 1894
(cat. no. 8)

NOTES

1. H. C. Bunner, "American Posters, Past and Present," *Scribner's Magazine* 18 (October 1895) as quoted in Carolyn Keay, *American Posters of the Turn of the Century* (New York: St. Martin's Press, 1975), 9.

2. Frank Luther Mott, "Magazine Revolution and Popular Ideas," *American Antiquarian Society Proceedings* 64 (April 1954): 197.

3. As referred to in Edgar Breitenbach, "A Brief History," *The American Poster* (New York: The American Federation of Arts, 1967), 12.

4. Will M. Clemens, *The Poster*, vol. 1, no. 2 (February, 1896): 16.

5. Roger Cunningham, "Cui Bono?," *Poster Lore*, book 1, part 4 (July 1896): 104.

6. Lionel Lambourne, "The Poster and the Popular Arts of the 1890s," *High Art and Low Life: The Studio and the Fin de Siècle*, vol. 201, no. 1022/1023 (1993): 18.

7. Maurice Talmeyer, "The Age of the Poster," *The Chautauquan* 24 (January 1897): 12-19, as quoted in Diane Chalmers Johnson, *American Art Nouveau* (New York: Harry N. Abrams, Inc., Publishers, 1979), 210.

8. Quoted in Clemens, *The Poster*, vol. 1, no. 1 (January 1896), unpaginated.

9. Sadakichi Hartmann, *A History of American Art*, vol. 2 (Boston: L. C. Page & Company, 1902), 131-32.

10. Will Bradley, "Edward Penfield, Artist," *Bradley, His Book*, vol. 1, no. 1 (May 1896), unpaginated.

11. Cunningham, 103.

12. Charles T. J. Hiatt, "The Collecting of Posters. A New Field for Connoisseurs," *The Studio*, vol. 1, no. 2 (May 1893): 61-62.

13. Ibid., 62.

14. Claude Fayette Bragdon, "Hereafter followeth the nature and tenor of this said book and the first part is the importance of design with a note on the absence of humor in American posters," *Poster Lore*, book 1, part 3 (April 1896): 75.

15. Ibid., 74.

16. Frederic Thoreau Singleton, "Notes," *Poster Lore*, book 1, part 4 (July 1896): 121.

17. Diane Chalmers Johnson, *American Art Nouveau*, 178.

18. Frederick Winthrop Faxon, *Ephemeral Bibelots: A Bibliography of Modern Chap-Books and Their Imitators* (Boston: The Boston Book Company, 1903), 3.

19. The complete list and comments about those magazines, about which Faxon had heard but had never seen, is contained in the Faxon article cited above, pp. 3-26.

20. For a complete description of the poster contest sponsored by *The Century*, see David W. Kiehl, *American Art Posters of the 1890s in the Metropolitan Museum of Art, including the Leonard A. Lauder Collection* (New York: The Metropolitan Museum of Art; distributed by Harry N. Abrams, New York, 1987), 14-15.

21. See Will Clemens, *The Poster*, vol. 1, no. 2 (February 1896): 15. "The living poster show is one of the social fads in Chicago, this winter. Even the churches there are given to living poster entertainments."

22. *The Poster*, ibid.

23. Joseph Goddu, *American Art Posters of the 1890s* (New York: Hirschl & Adler Galleries, 1990), 59.

24. As quoted in Edgar Breitenbach, "The Poster Craze," *American Heritage*, vol. 13, no. 2 (February 1962): 30. The date of 1896 for Hubbard's quote is given by Breitenbach without source and is repeated in Diane Chalmers Johnson, *American Art Nouveau*, 178. The 1896 date must certainly be mistaken as the editors of *The Chap-Book* replied to Hubbard's comments in their issue of July 1, 1895. Thus, in all likelihood, Hubbard's commentary was made in 1895.

25. "Notes," *The Chap-Book* (July 1, 1895): 159.

26. Peter Morse, "The American Poster Period: 1893-1897," *Auction Magazine*, vol. 3 (October 1969): 24.

27. S. C. De Soissons, "Ethel Reed and Her Art," *The Poster* (November 1898), as quoted in Carolyn Keay, *American Posters of the Turn of the Century* (New York: St. Martin's Press, 1975), 17.

28. Victor Margolin, *American Poster Renaissance* (New York: Watson-Guptill Publications, 1975), 29.

29. Jack Rennert, *Poster Potpourri* (New York: Poster Auctions International, 1988), 282.

30. Charles Hiatt, "Pictorial Book Advertisements in America," *The Poster and Art Collector*, vol. 6, as quoted in Carolyn Keay, *American Posters of the Turn of the Century* (New York: St. Martin's Press, 1975), 25.

31. *The Poster*, vol. 1, no. 4 (April 1896): 49, as noted in Kiehl, 133.

32. Examples of furniture by The Roycrofters are included in the Virginia Museum's collection, while Hubbard's books comprise part of the Museum Library's Rare Book Collection.

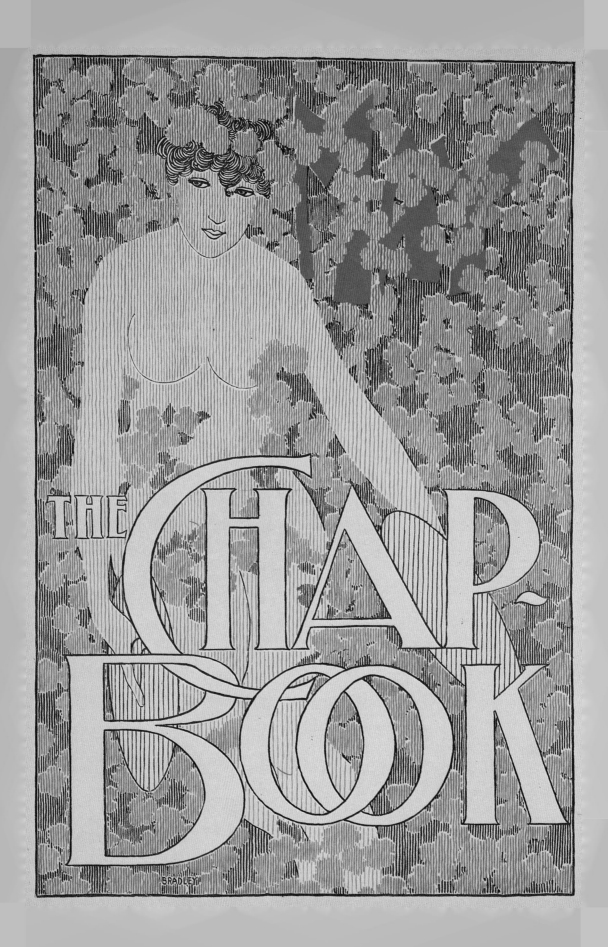

CHAPTER 2
Signs of the Times: The Artists

by Robert Koch

Figure 2.1. The American poster artist Will Bradley used color, line, and decorative elements to create his masterful poster designs. By age 26 the young designer was proclaimed "best in America." For this mysterious and provocative poster, he deftly juggled a fascinating interplay of figure and ground, subtle line work, and warm-cool colors. The nude, a daring image for a commercial poster, is nearly concealed by foliage, while the camouflaged issue title, "May," challenges the reader's visual perception. (A color sketch for this poster is in the collection of the Metropolitan Museum of Art, New York.)

Will H. Bradley
The Chap Book, May 1895 (cat. no. 13)

Nineteenth-century America saw the production of many advertising and circus posters, mostly made up by printers and lithographers, with very little value as works of art.[1] A change took place during the last decade of that century with the advent of posters designed by artists. This book deals with such posters, which were avidly collected, highly prized, and frequently exhibited at the time.

The collecting of posters as original prints began in France in the 1880s. In 1884 Ernest Maindron, already a collector of French posters, wrote an article for the *Gazette des Beaux-Arts,* "Les affiches illustrées," which was expanded and published as a book of the same title two years later.[2] In both the article and the book, Maindron gave the highest praise to the French artist Jules Chéret **(see figure 3.6,** p.41).

Meanwhile, in America, the discovery of posters as works of art began when *Harper's Magazine* commissioned Eugène Grasset, a Swiss-born illustrator working in Paris, to design posters for their 1889 Thanksgiving and Christmas issues. These, like his Christmas 1892 poster **(figure 2.2)**, were printed in Paris. Grasset also designed posters for the *Century Magazine* in 1894, 1895, and 1898.

In November 1890, the Grolier Club of New York organized an exhibition of posters, mainly French.[3] Then, in April 1893, *Harper's* began a series of posters appearing monthly and designed by American illustrator Edward Penfield, who was born in Brooklyn, New York, in 1866 and studied at the Art Students League. The campaign for *Harper's* lasted nearly a decade, resulting in Penfield's becoming one of America's most prolific poster artists **(see cat. nos. 64–77)**. Many of his best designs show the influence of Théophile-Alexandre Steinlen, a native of Switzerland who moved to Paris in 1882 and remained active there throughout his professional career.

In a book published in London in 1895, Charles Hiatt described Penfield's posters: "This artist's work is always ingeniously conceived, and the colour schemes are not seldom pleasantly audacious. Mr.

25

Figure 2.3. The prolific American artist Edward Penfield often featured images of fashionable and attractive young ladies in his poster designs.

Edward Penfield
Harper's June, 1899 (cat. no. 76)

Figure 2.2. *Harper's* was the first American publisher to realize the value of artistic posters to help promote their magazine, beginning with the commission of several designs by the noted Swiss-born illustrator Eugène Grasset in 1889.

Eugène Grasset
Harper's Magazine, Christmas 1892.
Collection of Dr. and Mrs. Robert Koch.

Penfield gives us very agreeable versions of the American girl in general, and of the 'summer girl' in particular **(figure 2.3)**. His maidens are adorably conscious of their power to charm, and are fully alive to the fact that their gowns are of the smartest."[4] A year later, in the first issue of his "little magazine," the artist Will Bradley included a tribute to Edward Penfield in which he wrote, "Mr. Penfield's work is wholly his own. It represents a thought; an expression; a mode of treatment which belongs to him alone; there is backbone to it. No matter what the pose, no matter what the idea, behind it all there is life, there is drawing, and good drawing. This alone marks him a master; and in methods of reproduction, that difficult point to which so few give even a passing thought, he is a past-master. . . . And just a word about his ideas. They are always timely, sparkling with wit, and in every way happy conceits. His color is delightful, strong and fresh, his treatment dainty. . . . For all reasons named, he stands first among designers of posters in America today.[5]

Two other poster artists continued Penfield's approach with emphasis on a simplified female figure representing the "new woman," and each made a series of designs for Lippincott's in Philadelphia. They were Will Carqueville, born in 1871, and J. J. Gould, a native of Philadelphia who continued the tradition after Carqueville left to study in Paris.

During that same time, another artist who was contributing to the development of the American poster was Louis J. Rhead. Born in Great Britain in 1857 and educated at the South Kensington Art School, Rhead visited Paris, where he met Grasset, and emigrated to the United States in 1883. His first posters, in a style derived from both Grasset and the English pre-Raphaelites, were created for *The Century* and *Harper's Bazaar.*

In 1892 Walter Crane, another English graphic artist and designer whose illustrated books for children were already well known, made a lecture tour of the United States. In the audience at his appearance in Chicago was the young Will Bradley, born in Boston in 1868. At the time, Bradley was working in Chicago for *The Inland Printer,* but it was not until two years later, in August 1894, that he designed his first poster, "The Twins," for *The Chap-Book,* published by Stone and Kimball **(see figure 1.25)**. This was the first of a series of seven posters to promote the new pocket-sized literary periodical, which was the first of its kind. Bradley's style was more varied and more creative than that of any other American artist **(see figure 2.1)**. The only influence that can be identified in his work at this time seems to have come from the English illustrator Aubrey Beardsley, whose work could be seen in the pages of *The Chap-Book* and on the shelves of local book collectors. The clearest example can be seen in Bradley's poster *When Hearts are Trumps* **(figure 2.4)**, which derives from a Beardsley illustration for Oscar Wilde's *Salomé* **(figure 3.8)**. But there is a basic difference between the two artists' styles. Bradley's design emphasizes the linear, decorative quality of the design, without the emotional symbolism that appears in most of Beardsley's work. Charles Hiatt recognized this fact and he explained it as follows: "It will hardly be disputed that he has seen and assimilated, in no small degree, the manner of Mr. Aubrey Beardsley. He is, however, a great deal more than a mere imitator; what he has borrowed he has borrowed with conspicuous intelligence, and nobody could for a moment accuse him of anything approaching petty larceny."[6] In December 1894, when the Bradley family was preparing to move from Chicago to Springfield, Massachusetts, an article was published in the *Chicago Sunday Tribune* claiming that Bradley was "the best in America. No one else has such a wealth of invention, so clear and flowing a line; no one else makes an equally conscientious effort to get the best decorative effect out of an inch square initial or poster covering half the street. . . . Bradley discovered for himself how to place strange but effective

Figure 2.4. The illustrative style of English artist Aubrey Beardsley, especially as seen in his illustrations for Oscar Wilde's *Salomé* **(see figure 3.8)**, strongly influenced the younger American artist Will Bradley.

Will Bradley
When Hearts are Trumps,
December 1894,
Collection of Dr. and Mrs. Robert Koch.

Figure 2.5. After working with Will Bradley in Chicago during the 1880s, W. W. Denslow went on to collaborate with Elbert Hubbard, founder of The Roycrofters, an aesthetic movement in East Aurora, New York. Many of Denslow's satirical drawings appeared on the back covers of various issues of Hubbard's magazine, *The Philistine.*

William W. Denslow
Books to Burn, August 1898, Collection of Dr. and Mrs. Robert Koch.

Figure 2.6. *The Poster,* one of the earliest of many specialized "little magazines," rode atop the crest of the poster craze of the 1890s. Will M. Clemens for Redfield Brothers, New York, volume 1, number 2, February 1896 edition of *The Poster.* Cover illustration by Louis J. Rhead reproduced "from a book catalogue" published by The Century Company, Collection of Dr. and Mrs. Robert Koch.

blacks, how to weave them with delicate lines into a harmonious drawing, how to enrich them with lavish and skillful ornament."[7] Then, in 1896, more words of praise were published by his mentor, Walter Crane. "Another artist of considerable invention and decorative ability has recently appeared in America, Mr. Will H. Bradley, whose designs for 'The Inland Printer' of Chicago are remarkable for careful and delicate line-work, and effective treatment of black and white, and showing the influence of the newer English school with a Japanese blend."[8]

Will Bradley's posters of 1894–95 introduced the Art Nouveau style to the United States and had a profound effect on several of his contemporaries, including William W. Denslow, Frank Hazenplug, Claude Bragdon, and Elisha Brown Bird. Denslow knew Bradley in Chicago in the 1880s and they collaborated on some book illustrations published in 1890. More than four years later, when Bradley moved to Springfield, Massachusetts, Denslow began to work with Elbert Hubbard in East Aurora, New York **(figure 2.5)**. Both Hazenplug and Bragdon contributed to *The Chap-Book* and continued to make posters for this publication in Chicago after Bradley left. Bird made posters for magazines published in Boston and New York.

The immediate success of *The Chap-Book* resulted in the publication of other "little magazines," in cities from coast to coast. January 1895 saw the first issue of *The Bibelot,* published by Thomas B. Mosher in Portland, Maine; the first issue of *The Lark* was published by William Doxey in San Francisco on May 1, 1895; *Chips* was first published in New York, May 1895; the first copy of *The Philistine* appeared in June 1895 in East Aurora, New York; *The Poster* by Will M. Clemens **(figure 2.6)** was issued in New York City in January 1896; and Will Bradley created his own "little magazine," which he titled *Bradley, His Book,* in Springfield, Massachusetts. Volume 1, Number 1, was completed April 25, 1896.[9] Like the "little magazines" and the posters created to publicize them, poster collections grew like wildfire in the 1890s. One collection belonging to Wilbur C. Whitehead in Cleveland, Ohio was listed in December 1895 in a privately printed catalogue of cover designs and posters that ran more than fifty pages and included several hundred items, of which forty-seven were by Will Bradley.

Most of the posters completed in the first half of the 1890s were in the flat, curvilinear style of early Art Nouveau.[10] Later, a more painterly approach can be seen in the posters by the American artist Ethel Reed **(figure 2.7)**, who was influenced by the French painter Henri de Toulouse-Lautrec, and in posters by such painters as J. H. Twachtman **(figure 2.8)** and Maxfield Parrish. This less linear, more painterly quality is also reflected in some of the later works by Edward Penfield.

Early recognition of the importance of such posters can be seen in several books published during the period. The first American example is *The Modern Poster,* issued with both frontispiece and poster by Will Bradley, and *Posters in Miniature,* with an introduction by Edward Penfield.[11]

Recognition of posters was equally swift abroad. In 1895 in England, Charles Hiatt's *Picture Posters* was published by George Bell,

Figure 2.7. After around 1894, a number of artists began to take a freer, more painterly approach to their images.

Ethel Reed
Fairy Tales, 1895 (cat. no. 85)

Figure 2.8. A more relaxed, free-flowing drawing style can be seen in the work of several poster artists during the second half of the 1890s.

John H. Twachtman
The Damnation of Theron Ware, 1896, Collection of Dr. and Mrs. Robert Koch.

Figure 2.9. This poster of 1898 by W. W. Denslow signals the end of the Art Nouveau-style poster movement. Posters of the decades that followed would be designed in a more realistic, narrative style.

William W. Denslow
The Home Magazine, August 1898
(cat. no. 32)

with a simultaneous American edition by Macmillan **(see figure 1.5, p.4)**. In 1896, Bell published Walter Crane's *Decorative Illustration*; and in June 1898, the first number of *The Poster* appeared on the newsstands of London. An article, "The American Poster," was included in the August 1898 issue.

American posters were first recognized in Paris in December 1895 when S. Bing opened his Salon de l'Art Nouveau and included several of Bradley's posters in the premiere exhibition. In the next few years, American posters continued to be recognized abroad. A chapter on posters in the United States was included in the 1897 French publication *Les affiches etrangères illustrées,* and several Americans were featured in *Les maîtres de l' affiche.*[12] In addition, from April to May 1897, Louis Rhead had a one-man show at the Salon des Cent in Paris.

After moving to Springfield, Massachusetts, in 1896, Will Bradley completed seven issues of *Bradley, His Book* (**figure 1.16**) before suffering physical collapse from overwork in 1897 (**see cat. nos. 8-21**). During the interim, he had designed more than half a dozen posters for himself and local clients, and had printed a few books as well. He eventually moved to Concord, and finally, after the turn of the century, to New Jersey. In 1900 he became art director of *Collier's Weekly*, for which he designed many covers in a style suggestive of the work of Maxfield Parrish. Bradley later worked for William Randolph Hearst and as a free-lancer was the highest paid commercial artist in the United States.[13] He continued to work as an illustrator and type designer past his eightieth birthday, and died at the age of ninety-four in 1962.[14]

One of Bradley's colleagues, William W. Denslow (**figure 2.9**), achieved great success as the illustrator of L. Frank Baum's *The Wonderful Wizard of Oz* in 1899. He continued to write and to illustrate children's books until his death in 1915. Likewise many of the artists whose posters were so popular and successful in the 1890s—including Maxfield Parrish, Louis Rhead, and Edward Penfield—continued to work as illustrators in the twentieth century. But after 1898, with the outbreak of the Spanish-American War, the poster movement associated with the Art Nouveau style came to an end. The First World War (1914–1918) produced a new crop of poster artists working in a very different style, one that employed more realistic representation in an illustrative manner. ▣

NOTES

1. Mary Black, *American Advertising Posters of the Nineteenth Century* (New York: Dover, 1976).

2. Ernest Maindron, "Les affiches illustrées," *Gazette des Beaux-Arts* 30 (1884): 419-433; and *Les affiches illustrées* (Paris, 1886). In 1896 he published a sequel, *Les affiches illustrées 1886-1895*.

3. The Grolier Club exhibition included 38 posters by Chéret, 5 by Grasset, and a few characteristic American examples.

4. Charles Hiatt, *Picture Posters* (London: George Bell, 1895), 288.

5. Will Bradley, "Edward Penfield, Artist," *Bradley, His Book*, vol. 1, no. 1 (May 1896): 18, 19.

6. Hiatt, 298.

7. "Will Bradley, Artist," *Chicago Sunday Tribune*, December 30, 1894, p. 1.

8. Walter Crane, *Decorative Illustration* (London and New York: George Bell, 1896), 274-78.

9. Robert Koch, "Artistic Books, Periodicals and Posters of the 'gay' nineties," *The Art Quarterly*, vol. 25, no. 4 (Winter 1962): 370-83.

10. Robert Koch, "The Poster Movement and 'Art Nouveau'," *Gazette des Beaux-Arts* 50 (1957): 285-96.

11. See *The Modern Poster* (New York: Scribner's, 1895) and *Posters in Miniature* (New York: R. H. Russell, 1896).

12. See *Les affiches etrangères illustrées* (Paris: G. Boudet, 1897) and *Les maîtres de l'affiche* (Paris: Imprimeries Chaix, 1896-99).

13. Author unidentified (E.G.G.), "Sketches and Impressions of an American Printer," *The American Printer*, January 20, 1924, pp. 42-46.

14. Will Bradley, *Will Bradley, His Chap-Book* (New York: The Typophiles, 1955); see also Robert Koch, "Will Bradley," *Art in America* 3 (1962): 78-83.

HARPER'S WEEKLY

NATIONAL AUTHORITY
ON AMATEUR SPORT

CHAPTER 3
Turn-of-the-Century American Posters: Art + Technology = Graphic Design

by Philip B. Meggs

During the nineteenth century, the Industrial Revolution changed human society from a rural, agrarian culture, dependent on the power of man and beast, to an urban manufacturing society, based on technology and machines. With this shift, all aspects of the human condition, from work and leisure to transportation and communication, were irrevocably altered. In response to several simultaneous changes—a rising tide of literacy, the expansion of marketing and manufacturing, and astounding innovations in printing machines and methods—printed information took on new roles. Ultimately, the impact of aesthetic, cultural, and technological forces gave birth to a new profession: graphic design (**figure 3.1**).

The Poster in Context

In Chapter 1 of this book, we read how Americans quickly developed an enthusiasm for the new graphic images they saw in posters. Arsène Alexandre called it "poster mania."[1] What aspects of the American national character made the late nineteenth-century phenomenon so acute? H. C. Bunner had observed that, "the craving to look at pictures, or even decorative lettering or pure decoration itself, seems to be natural to all types and classes of Americans"[2] (**figure 3.2**).

Traveling circuses, which reached the height of their popularity at the end of the nineteenth century, fueled Americans' love of posters. Over one hundred troupes crisscrossed the country, announcing their impending arrivals with large-scale posters printed in vibrant, primary colors. "Certain old Puritanical traditions [led Americans to look at pictorial art as] idle vanities; and even had this prejudice been less general, the sources of artistic supply were meagre in the extreme."[3] This scarcity of pictures combined with the "utilitarian character [of circus and advertising posters to give] them a sort of right to a place on the walls of the barn."[4]

As utilitarian messages relating to commerce, posters appealed to Americans' pragmatic mercantile nature. The central role of business

Figure 3.1. Late nineteenth-century advances in print technology and an aesthetic concern for color, form, and type are both apparent in this sophisticated poster design by Maxfield Parrish.

Maxfield Parrish
Harper's Weekly, 1896 (cat. no. 61)

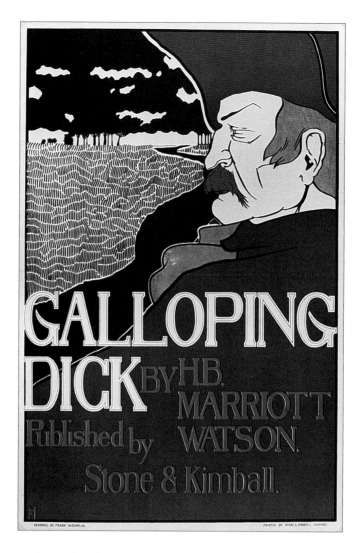

Figure 3.2. The Americans' love of adventure can be seen in this tightly designed poster, which combines the image of a swashbuckling highwayman with the bold overlap of graphic text.

Frank Hazenplug
Galloping Dick, 1896 (cat. no. 45)

activity (and creative disorder) in nineteenth-century American life was observed by journalist George W. Steevens, dispatched from England by the *London Daily Mail* to cover the 1896 presidential elections: "Business is business all the world over; so, at least, I have been assured by those who ought to know. But it is more emphatically business in the United States than in anywhere else. . . . Cut off from the hard-won civilization of the Old World, and left to struggle by themselves with the forest and the prairie, it was inevitable that the Americans should prize most highly those less highly organized qualities of the mind which insured success in the struggle."[5]

Many Europeans viewed the United States as a cultural wasteland offering but little support for the arts. When world-renowned composer Antonín Dvořák was asked by *Harper's New Monthly* to comment on the state of American culture, he responded, "When I see how much is done in every other field by public-spirited men in America—how schools, universities, libraries, museums, hospitals, and parks spring up out of the ground and are maintained by generous gifts—I can only marvel that so little has been done for music. . . . The great American republic alone, in its national government as well as in the several governments of the states, suffers art and music to go without encouragement."[6] The American public's embrace of poster art at the turn of the century occurred at least in part because it satisfied people's craving for visual aesthetic experiences, yet it achieved legitimacy in the plebeian American society because of its functional, commercial role, thereby avoiding the stigma of "art for art's sake."

The New Possibilities in Print Technology

During the 1880s and 1890s, technological advances in printing dramatically changed the graphic arts. These changes played an indispensable role in expanding the technical and expressive possibilities for designers and illustrators, and, in the end, made the poster revolution possible. Photoengraving—whereby photographic and chemical processes were combined to create line engravings, halftones, and lithographic plates from the artist's original work **(figure 3.1)**— replaced the labor-intensive process of making a printing plate by hand. The number of steps and the number of people between artist and printed image was reduced, and this ultimately gave the artist greater control.

Before the poster revolution of the 1890s, many American posters revealed little originality or beauty. The typical American poster featured a tightly rendered tonal illustration and suffered from a general lack of design unity between the lettering and the image. It appears from accounts of the time that both artists and printing craftsmen harbored attitudes that worked against the creation of more artistic posters. The "artist or designer considered himself above his task when he was working on these 'advertisements,' and failed to produce a successful poster because he failed to realize that he was engaged either in a difficult problem, or one worthy of his best efforts."[7] Conversely, the artisan-draftsmen, who copied the artist's work onto the lithographic stones, were usually highly skilled Germans, trained in strictly disciplined Bavarian technical schools, and possessing "an enduring force of character only to be found elsewhere in the mule and the martyr at the stake."[8] These draftsmen duplicated the artist's image on lithographic printing stones with meticulous crayon and tusche stipple techniques, requiring hours of painstaking work. The "lithographic draughtsman had very little use for art, and a profound contempt for the artist. . . ."[9] This attitude resulted in a "perverse conservatism that for many years prevailed against the efforts of every artist who tried to do anything new and bold in the use of flat tints, or new forms of modelling in designing of posters. . . ."[10]

The American tendency to devote "energies [in poster production] almost entirely to the mechanical side—to processes of reproduction rather than to the artistic consideration of what he was producing"[11] resulted in posters that "cannot be taken seriously; and verge[s] upon the impossible when considered in any connection with the tenets of abstract art. Not only were the most fundamental principles of poster design, as such, ignored, but the principles of design of any kind seem to have formed no part of these first essays in a new field."[12]

H. C. Bunner had found "something pitiful in this attempt to satisfy a natural appetite with the very lowest form of pictorial artifice; and a serious mischief sprang from it in the damper it put on any development or progress in the art of poster designs. It became an understood

thing that the general public would not have anything better than the flashy and ill executed prints to which they had grown accustomed; and year after year the same old pictorial horrors were scattered [across] city and country."[13]

Turn-of-the-century posters were a technological continuation of— and a vigorous aesthetic reaction against—the primary poster printing method of the 1860s to the 1880s: chromolithography. Lithography, invented by the Bavarian Aloys Senefelder in 1796, is based on the simple principle that oil and water do not mix. The image to be printed is drawn or painted onto a smooth, flat stone in an oil-based medium. The stone is moistened with water, which wets the stone but is repelled by the oily image. When an oil-based ink is applied to the stone surface with a roller, it adheres to the oily surface of the image, but not to the moistened stone. Chromolithography is a color lithographic printing process in which a series of stones are printed using as many as 30 ink colors. The process required precise alignment of the separate stones, called registration, but also made remarkable strides in speed and economy. Beginning in the 1860s, the transition from hand presses to steam-powered presses allowed significant increases in output. A competent craftsman operating a hand lithographic press could produce "200 to 250 impressions in a twelve-hour workday,"[14] while advertisements for steam-powered Hoe presses claimed a capacity of 1,310 impressions per hour.[15] The economies that resulted from numerous innovations produced an outpouring of colorful postcards, greeting cards, art prints, posters, and advertising trade cards. Chromolithographs became a form of visual art for every person, including those of the working class, who previously did not have access to colorful printed images.

During most of the nineteenth century, books were bound with neutral or subdued cover sheets of grey, yellow, blue, or pink paper and only had the title and the names of the author and the publisher printed on them. Each magazine had a standard cover design every month, typically an ornate masthead over a listing of the issue's contents, printed in black ink on a colored paper stock. During the middle 1880s, the French publisher Jules Lévy is credited with first observing the possible link between the chromolithographic poster and the book jacket.[16] It was Lévy who prevailed upon Jules Chéret, justifiably honored as "the father of the modern poster,"[17] to design color lithographic jackets for his books. Although Lévy's publishing enterprise failed, his vision of colorful illustrated bookjackets was taken up by other publishers on both sides of the Atlantic, transforming the bookstalls of Europe and America.

Magazines also began to feature illustrated covers. The American poster designer Will Bradley recounted his 1894 conversation with a Mr. McQuilkin, editor of *The Inland Printer,* who had commissioned Bradley to create a permanent cover for the magazine:

> When [the] design is finished I ask:
> "Why not a series of covers—a change of design with every issue?"
> "Can't afford them."
> "How about my making an inducement in the way of a tempting price?"
> "I'll take the suggestion to Shephard."
> Suggestion approved by Henry O. Shephard, printer and publisher, and the series is started—an innovation, the first occasion when a monthly magazine changes its cover design with every issue[18] **(figure 3.3).**

The jump from monthly cover design to a monthly poster to advertise the magazine was made quickly: Bradley's newest covers for *The Inland Printer* were reprinted with copy in the margins above and below announcing the availability of the latest issue.

Another technological change led to the popularization of poster images. The efficiency of high-speed, steam-powered rotary presses caused the price of printing to plunge. In 1845, printing a thousand copies of a three-sheet poster had required 75 man-hours with a labor cost of $9.75. But by 1896 a similar three-sheet poster could be printed with only 6 hours and 50 minutes of labor costing $1.59.[19]

Typesetting was also mechanized in the late 1880s, when the keyboard-operated Linotype and Monotype machines began to replace the slow, laborious process of setting type by hand. The February 1899 issue of *The Inland Printer* reported that Frank Bevan, Linotype operator for the Sydney (Australia) *Daily Telegraph,* had been able to set eleven full columns of type in an eight-hour shift; it would have required about two full weeks of solid work to set this amount of type by hand.[20] Estimates of time and wage savings by machine-set typography vary widely; however, an 1896 study by the U.S. Bureau of Labor shows an eight-fold reduction in typesetting time and a ten-fold reduction in labor costs. A typesetting job that would have required 148 hours of labor at a cost of $41.60 if set by hand was completed by a keyboard-operated typesetting machine in 17 hours and 20 minutes, requiring a labor expense of only $4.40.[21] Wage costs for printing 10,000 copies of a 64-page magazine had been $302.50 on a hand press in 1852; by 1896 the same press run required a mere $4.63 in wage expenses.[22] Yet dire predictions of widespread unemployment did not materialize, for with the advances allowed by machine technology, rapid economic expansion also occurred.

When the production costs of books, magazines, and newspapers plunged downward, a spiral of lower prices resulted, which created a higher volume of sales. The resulting increase in circulation attracted more advertising, which permitted even lower prices and even greater production economy, spurring even higher circulation, and so on. This rapid expansion of the publishing industry caused the poster movement to flourish as publishers commissioned posters and pictorial cover designs in a vigorous competition for readers. Magazines and books became major users of illustrators and designers; and "the periodical publications of America began to develop the illustrator into a responsible and respectable artist."[23]

New Aesthetics in Poster Design

The conditions created by new technology made possible the evolution toward more artistic posters, but these same conditions did not account for the aesthetic revolution that occurred. The aesthetic vision for American posters and other printed matter of the 1860s to the 1880s has a Teutonic origin. Germany's Düsseldorf Academy of Art, with its rigorous curriculum of traditional academic drawing, trained many German artists who, after immigrating to America, created images that were meant to be reproduced by chromolithography.[24] Henry Tuckerman's critique of Düsseldorf art seems relevant to the style of chromolithographic posters before the 1890s: "*Knowingness* may be considered the special trait of this class of artists; they are often excellent draughtsmen, expert, like all artistic Germans, in form and composition, but in color [they are] frequently hard and dry; they abound in the intellectual, and are wanting in the sensuous. . . . Skill prevails over imagination."[25]

An overarching influence on the aesthetic of the day was the excitement Western artists and designers felt when they first encountered Japanese prints. This influence began as early as 1865, when English artist and designer Walter Crane "accidentally met a young naval officer, just returned from the land of the rising sun. Among the curios collected by this officer on his cruise was a sheaf of Japanese colour-prints, some of which passed into the possession of the young

Figure 3.4. Many early American poster designs drew inspiration from the flat, simple compositions of the Japanese print, which also influenced European artists of the day.

Arthur Wesley Dow
The Lotos, 1896 (cat. no. 35)

artist, who was greatly struck by their decorative beauty. The toy-books by Walter Crane, published a year or two after this occurrence, show the consummate skill with which he knew how to account the teaching of the artists of Japan."[26] Until the late nineteenth century, American and European posters had always reflected the values of traditional Italian Renaissance art: following the best Renaissance models, they tended to present a series of narrative events in illusionistic shadow-box space, illuminated by an imaginary fixed light source that rendered forms as in three-dimensions, through strong light-and-shadow contrasts. Japanese prints, on the other hand, presented their subjects in flat planes of color, with stylized linear contours, and among a series of flat, rhythmic patterns. Here, the image was not a story or a representation of outward appearances; rather, it becomes a concept, sign, or symbol. This cross-cultural influence from East to West enabled poster designers and illustrators, as well as painters such as James A. McNeill Whistler, to reinvent their art as a conscious arrangement of carefully chosen elements. The resulting abstraction made the turn-of-the-century poster *proto-modern,* pointing the way toward twentieth-century modern art.

The Japanese influence invaded American graphics by way of French and English mentors when, in the early 1890s, American poster designers drew inspiration from their immediate European predecessors. "It was left to the French to show the world how much of beauty and of inspiration could enter into the poster, and it was many years before the designing world at large learned its lesson (if indeed, it may yet be said to have been learned) from the daring, sparkling sheets of flaming color that have decorated the streets of Paris."[27]

The visual attributes of the Japanese print satisfied the functional purposes of the Western poster. The fact that the poster would need to be viewed from a distance made the use of flat areas of color, simplified drawing, and strong silhouettes an ideal approach to poster design **(figure 3.4).** The Japanese style also helped poster designers to confront the same obstacles that Walter Crane considered a major impediment when he wrote: "The jostling together of conflicting scenes and motives on the hoarding, however, to which all must submit, is as inartistic a condition of things as a picture exhibition. The very fact of the necessity of shouting aloud, and the association with vulgar commercial puffing, are against the artist and so much dead weight."[28] By the mid 1890s, as poster design evolved under the Japanese design influences, M. H. Spielmann believed that "'shouting' is no longer necessary . . . the artistic poster of real beauty proclaims itself gently, but irresistibly, out of the mass of kaleidoscopic color and common design. Few colors in strong contrast skillfully arranged, the fewest lines and masses, simple chiaroscuro, added to charm, dignity, or vigor of design—these are the elements and essentials; and if the conditions are properly fulfilled the result is an artistic triumph of which any artist might be proud."[29] The nineteenth-century American poster designer Edward Penfield observed how difficult it was to achieve simplicity when he quoted one of the partners in Beggarstaffs, a London poster-design pair, as saying, "Our designs may not look as if much time was spent upon them, but I can assure you that it has taken all the artistic knowledge we possess to bring them to the simple state in which you see them."[30]

"Some posters," Penfield added, "consisting of but a few lines and containing but a few broad masses of color, require a dozen drawings before simplicity and harmony of color are obtained"[31] (figure 3.5).

In many Japanese prints, a large central figure interacts with the surrounding space; not as a dimensional form in a three-dimensional environment, but as a flat shape in a dynamic two-dimensional spatial relationship with other shapes. This simple compositional idea is one of the most pervasive influences on turn-of-the-century posters. The Japanese prints that began to influence artists in the late nineteenth century inspired a design wholeness as designers consciously worked to blend two disparate means of conveying visual information—verbally with words and pictorially with images—into a visual unity. Their images comprised two-dimensional line, shape, and color, rather than tonally modelled three-dimensional illusions. In so doing, designers unified the formal characteristics of lettering and illustrations. Poster artists now had greater latitude when organizing different elements into a unified composition.

Two extremes of poster expression—marking the boundaries between which most other European and American poster designers worked—were found in the work of French poster designer Jules Chéret and the [evil] incantations of the tubercular young English artist, Aubrey Beardsley. Chéret designed more than a thousand posters, enlivening French hoardings with his vibrant color and joyously happy maidens (figure 3.6). According to critic Charles Hiatt, Chéret's body of work possessed "no decorative forerunners; it is not a thing derived; its parents are the gaieties of modern Paris."[32] His work was "infused with a somewhat hectic gaiety which holds a not unimportant place in the lives of us suffering from this 'sick disease of modern life.' Of the sick disease itself, Chéret gives no hint. He is unflagging in his vivacity, unswerving in his insistence on the *joie de vivre*."[33] Chéret's contemporaries believed he played a major role in establishing the artistic integrity of "a branch of art until quite recently despised and held of little moment,"[34] for the "judicious, as soon as their eyes fell upon Chéret's vast lithographs, decided that he was no mere colour-printer's hack, but an artist whose work would have to be reckoned with."[35]

Beardsley, according to his contemporary M. H. Speilmann, was "a draughtsman of weird and singular power, who, after importing into his art elements so suggestively opposite as his distorted echoes of Chinese or Annamite execution and Rossettian feeling, seen with a squinting eye, imagined with a Mephistophelian brain, and executed with a vampire hand, showed a deep natural instinct for the beauty of line, for the balance of chiaroscuro, and for decorative effect. It was the aesthetic craze of an earlier day run mad—startlingly novel, original, and *spirituel,* [sic] and full of artistic cleverness."[36]

Figure 3.5. Edward Penfield's eloquently simple designs belied the many sketches and revisions that went into the creation of each poster's final design.

Edward Penfield
Harper's September, 1896
(cat. no. 67)

Figure 3.6. In 1895, French poster designer Jules Chéret was described by the American poster critic Charles Hiatt as "an artist whose work would have to be reckoned with." Chéret infused his images with the lighthearted, carefree ambiance of *"la gaieté parisienne,"* a mood that would eventually influence many American poster designs at the turn of the century.

Jules Chéret
Benzo-Moteur, late 1890s, Collection of the Virginia Museum of Fine Arts, Purchase, The Arthur and Margaret Glasgow Fund, accession no. 72.9.3.

Figure 3.7. Early designs by Will Bradley are enlivened by the same swirling lines and decorative foliage as were used by his English predecessor Aubrey Beardsley (**compare figure 3.8**).

Will H. Bradley
The Inland Printer, New Year's Number, circa 1894.

Figure 3.8. Aubrey Beardsley, "Peacock Skirt" from ***Salome*** by Oscar Wilde. London: Elkin Matthews, 1894.

The debt American poster artists owed to their French and English predecessors is evident when one compares early works by the American artist Will H. Bradley (**figure 3.7**) to those of the Englishman Aubrey Beardsley (**figure 3.8**), Louis Rhead (**figure 3.9**) to Eugène Grasset (**figure 3.10**), or Edward Penfield (**figure 3.11**) to Henri de Toulouse-Lautrec (**figure 3.12**).

H. C. Bunner must have had Bradley's early influence from Beardsley in mind when he wrote, in 1895, "But imitation is not so readily forgiven when it takes the form of even a conscientious Americanization of a brutal English parody on the eccentricities of mediaeval [sic] Florentine art; and it is pleasant to see that the artist who on our side of the water has most conspicuously shown cleverness in this re-adaptation is growing away from his British model and developing his own characteristic powers, which point him as naturally to lines of beauty as the qualities of the foreigner urge him to a morbid delight in the contortions of ugliness."[37] With Beardsley's inspiration as a launching pad, Bradley's work soon evolved into a singular and personal graphic statement.

The Poster as Social Phenomenon

As noted earlier, the aesthetic properties of turn-of-the-century posters led, in America as well as abroad, to what the French author, Arsène Alexandre, called "poster mania . . . [a] comparatively new disease— an excellent disease, by the way, for it furnishes material for some rich and curious collections; and one which has brought into being a whole branch of commerce and industry far from unimportant."[38] The "illness" first erupted among admirers of Jules Chéret's posters in France. Print-sellers arranged to purchase copies from bill-posters, but this process promptly ended in France when printers and artists brought suits one against the other and judicial penalties were issued. Print dealers began to buy portions of press runs specifically in order to sell them to collectors. Posters on special papers, posters without type, and posters in signed and numbered editions also became available.[39] Gallery and museum exhibitions of posters soon followed, and posters were eventually elevated to the status of fine-art prints. Collectors made it possible for the poster, an ephemeral form of public communication, to live long past its immediate time and its original function. A full century after the poster first erupted onto the cultural milieu, in the 1890s, turn-of-the-century posters are still being collected, exhibited, and critiqued.

Americans, long suffering under the stigma of cultural subservience to Europe, took great pride in the development of the poster art in their own country. As H. C. Bunner, the oft-quoted spokesman of poster commentary has observed, "Starting from a lower plane than French art ever knew, our [American] designers have reached a level of artistic equality with all except the acknowledged masters of this curious line of work in France or elsewhere; and there are evidences of the natural, healthy, unaffected growth of certain tendencies that must lead to the formation of a distinctly American school."[40]

Figure 3.9. American poster designer Louis Rhead apparently admired the figural compostions and draftsmanship of the Swiss poster designer Eugène Grasset.

Louis J. Rhead
L. Prang and Co.'s Holiday Publications, 1895 (cat. no. 95)

Figure 3.10. Eugène Grasset, design for the French Decorative Artist Exhibition at the Grafton Gallery, London, 1893. Reproduced from Charles Hiatt, ***Picture Posters*** (London: George Bell and Sons, 1895), 61.

Critics of the day sought to legitimize the uniqueness of the American accomplishment. In considering Edward Penfield's work, Bunner found:

> In the lightness, freshness, and purity of that humor; in the composition, free without license, and unconventional without extravagance; in the striking yet inoffensive use of color; in the frankness and unaffected innocence and happy simplicity of the whole thing, I find a quality which, I am grateful to think, comes to the American artist . . . as his natural and honest birthright.[41]

In response to the English literary and social critic Matthew Arnold, who complained that he found no "distinction" in American culture, novelist William Dean Howells, editor of *Atlantic Monthly* and *Harper's,* issued a challenge to all American arts in 1891: Americans, Howells said,

> have been now some hundred years building up a state on the affirmation of the essential equality of men in their rights and duties, and whether we have been right or wrong, the gods have taken us at our word and have responded to us with a civilization in which there is no

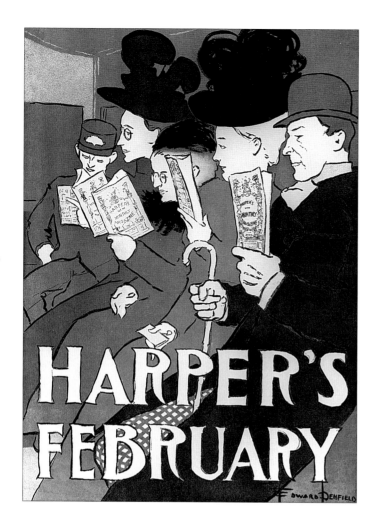

Figure 3.11. American poster designer Edward Penfield often created a greatly simplified image with lettering overlapping a diagonal progression of forms, a technique that had been effectively employed earlier by the noted French artist Henri de Toulouse-Lautrec.

Edward Penfield
Harper's February, 1897 (cat. no. 69)

Figure 3.12. Henri de Toulouse-Lautrec, ***Reine de Joie*** (Queen of Happiness), Paris: Edward Ancourt, 1892. Reproduced from Jack Rennert, *Posters of the Belle Epoque: The Wine Spectator Collection* (New York: Wine Spectator Press, 1990), with kind permission of the publisher.

'distinction' perceptible to the eye that loves and values it. Such beauty and grandeur as we have is common beauty, common grandeur. . . . It seems to me that these conditions invite the artist to the study and appreciation of the common, and to the portrayal in every art of those finer and higher aspects which unite rather than sever humanity, if he would thrive in our new order of things.

The talent that is robust enough to [confront] the everyday world and catch the charm of its workworn, careworn, brave, kindly face, need not fear the encounter. . . . The arts must become democratic, and then we shall have the expression of America in art; and the reproach which Mr. Arnold was half right in making us shall have no justice in it any longer; we shall be 'distinguished.'[42]

American posters of the turn of the century—through their accessibility to the public, their articulation of everyday life, and their stunning graphic vitality—became a distinguished expression of America in the visual arts. In large measure this explains the renown that such posters received in their time, and their enduring popularity as cultural artifacts.

As a direct result of this new generation of poster artists, a new attitude and philosophy emerged in American graphic arts. As the twentieth century unfolded, a distinct category of artistic activity emerged: the skilled renderer was replaced by aesthetically trained designers of printed matter who combined an understanding of graphic technology, a sense of visual organization and aesthetics, and a commitment to the communicative functions of the graphic message. Often, a personal point of view emerged. A defining moment occurred on August 29, 1922, when William Addison Dwiggins used the term "graphic design" in an article he wrote for the *Boston Evening Transcript* entitled, "New Kind of Printing Calls for New Kind of Design." A whole new art profession had been born in the halcyon days that spawned the turn-of-the-century poster, and now, it had a name: graphic design. ▣

NOTES

1. Arsène Alexandre, "French Posters and Book-Covers," *The Modern Poster* (New York: Charles Scribner's Sons, 1895), 23.

2. H. C. Bunner, "American Posters Past and Present" *The Modern Poster* (New York: Charles Scribner's Sons, 1895), 71.

3. Ibid., 71.

4. Ibid., 77.

5. George W. Steevens, *The Land of the Dollar* (New York: publisher unknown, 1897), 264-73.

6. Antonín Dvořák, "Music in America," *Harper's New Monthly* 90 (February 1895), 429-30.

7. Charles Matlack Price, *Poster Design: A Critical Study of the Development of the Poster in Continental Europe, England, and America,* new and enlarged edition (New York: George W. Bricka, 1913), 1.

8. Bunner, 89.

9. Ibid., 90.

10. Ibid., 91.

11. Price, 129.

12. Ibid., 129.

13. Bunner, 78.

14. Peter C. Marzio, *The Democratic Art: Pictures for a 19th-Century America* (Boston: David R. Godine, 1979), 80.

15. Ibid., 87.

16. Alexandre, 9-10.

17. Philip B. Meggs, *A History of Graphic Design,* 2nd ed. (New York: Van Nostrand Reinhold, 1992), 191.

18. Will H. Bradley, "Pictures of a Period, or Memories of the Gay Nineties and the Turn of the Century, also a Few of the Years that Followed," (Lecture to the Rounce and Coffin Club, location unknown, 1950), 9.

19. Elizabeth Faulkner Baker, *Printers and Technology* (Westport, Conn.: Greenwood Press, 1957), 22. Adapted from U.S. Bureau of Labor, *Hand and Machine Labor* (1898), I, 66-68; II, 1408-34.

20. George Lincoln, "Machine Composition Notes and Queries," *The Inland Printer* (Chicago: February, 1899).

21. Baker, 23.

22. Ibid., 22.

23. Bunner, 100.

24. For an excellent discussion of the Düsseldorf Academy's influence upon nineteenth-century American painting and chromolithography, see Chapter 3, "New York and Düsseldorf: Mecca and Inspiration," in Peter C. Marzio, *The Democratic Art: Pictures for a 19th-Century America* (Boston: David R. Godine, 1979), 41-48.

25. Henry T. Tuckerman, *Book of the Artists: American Artist Life* (New York: G. P. Putnam's Sons, 1867), 392.

26. P. G. Konody, *The Art of Walter Crane* (London: George Bell & Sons, 1902), 24-25.

27. Price, 1.

28. M. H. Spielmann, "Posters and Poster-Designing in England," *The Modern Poster* (New York: Charles Scribner's Sons, 1895), 65.

29. Ibid., 65-67.

30. Edward Penfield, *Posters in Miniature* (New York: R. H. Russell and Son, 1896), 1. The Beggarstaffs was the pseudonym for London poster artists James Pryde (1872-1949) and William Nicholson (1866-1941). Their brief partnership was active around 1894.

31. Ibid., 1.

32. Charles Hiatt, *Picture Posters* (London: George Bell and Sons, 1895), 30.

33. Ibid., 33.

34. Ibid., 29.

35. Ibid., 29.

36. Spielmann, 57.

37. Bunner, 98.

38. Alexandre, 23.

39. Ibid., 25-27.

40. Bunner, 96.

41. Ibid., 106.

42. William Dean Howells, *Criticism and Fiction* (New York, 1891; reprint, New York: New York University Press, 1959), 66-67.

THE ECHO

CHICAGO'S NEW PAPER :·:
·IN WHICH WILL APPEAR A SERIES·
OF COLORED FRONTISPIECES BY ·

WILL H. BRADLEY

FORTNIGHTLY   HUMOROUS AND
ARTISTIC ·:·

WILL H. BRADLEY.

CHAPTER 4
Technical Notes

by Philip B. Meggs

This sprightly sketch is probably one of several versions that the artist created as a small-scale preliminary drawing for a poster assignment.

Will H. Bradley
Preliminary drawing for "The Echo," circa 1894, watercolor, ink, pencil, and gouache on paper, 7 7/8 by 5 5/8 inches. Collection of David R. Anderson.

This large poster in four ink colors (yellow, red, blue, and black) appears to have been printed on letterpress. Its design follows almost exactly that of the sketch illustrated above.

Will H. Bradley
The Echo, 1895, letterpress, 21 1/4 by 14 1/2 inches (cat. no. 9)

From Artist's Vision to Printed Poster

How was an artist's original concept, such as Will Bradley's preliminary watercolor drawing for a poster (see illustration), transformed into a printed poster pasted all over Chicago to announce the city's new biweekly newspaper, *The Echo?* Based on information about design and printing that has survived over the decades, we can speculate about the events that occurred after the twice-monthly newspaper commissioned Bradley to design a poster.

Bradley probably made numerous small pencil sketches, called thumbnail sketches by graphic designers, until he felt the subject and composition of these miniature drawings represented an appropriate direction. Bradley may have decided to illustrate two young ladies holding hands with a moon and its reflection in the background to subtly signify the dual nature of an echo; or, he may have simply chosen this motif for its decorative design value. A careful yet freely drawn pencil sketch was made, emphasizing the flat planes and stylized curvilinear drawing that excited Bradley by 1894. We know that the twenty-six-year-old Bradley frequented the Chicago Public Library to devour European art magazines and had developed a wild enthusiasm for the work of the English illustrator Aubrey Beardsley. Bradley loosely brushed in flat areas of watercolor over the pencil drawing to explore tonal composition. Crisp outlines were drawn with a small pointed brush. Graphic designers often make numerous preliminary studies. Working against a tight deadline, the designer seeks a solution that successfully solves both the client's communications needs and satisfies the designer's aesthetic sense.

After Bradley felt he had solved the design problem, he probably presented several studies to his client for approval. With that approval, production details were finalized, including the number of colors to be printed, budget, printing method, and quantity. Bradley and his client agreed to produce the chosen design as a four-color poster in blue, red, yellow and black, and to print it on a letterpress.

Back in his studio, Bradley made a pen-and-ink line drawing of the primary image. By working on a textured paper, he was able to add a stipple pattern to areas of the line drawing by rubbing the raised surface with a tool capable of just marking the raised areas of the texture, either with a hard conté crayon or by using india ink with a stiff dry brush. This textured area created tonal variety in contrast to the linear drawing and flat color areas of the finished poster. This drawing was printed in blue ink and became the master art. It provided a guide for the red and yellow printed areas.

Many poster designers would draw the lettering as part of their illustration. This poster's title, *The Echo,* was hand-lettered directly onto the heavy paper in pen and ink. Bradley possessed great skill at hand-lettering; American Type Founders Company even produced a new typeface named "Bradley" based on lettering he designed for his magazine covers and posters. For the small type in the lower left section of the poster, metal type was set and proofed, then this type was printed in black ink over the other colors at the bottom of the poster.

By 1894, most letterpress posters were printed using photomechanical rather than hand-made printing plates; Bradley was an innovator in designing for photographic reproduction. The artist's final line drawing was delivered to the printing company, where it was placed on the copy board of a large engraver's camera and photographed, making a negative of the image. The advent of photographic printing processes freed artists from the need to work actual size. Illustrations to be reproduced in a small size could be drawn larger and reduced; images for very large posters could be drawn smaller than reproduction size then enlarged in the printer's camera. A 21 1/4-inch-tall poster like Bradley's *The Echo* was probably drawn actual reproduction size.

In a darkroom, the line negative was placed on a metal plate coated with a light-sensitive emulsion, then it was exposed to light. Photographic processing hardened the exposed area and the unexposed emulsion was washed away. The metal plate was then placed in an acid bath, which etched away the raw metal, leaving a raised image.

Craftsmen at the printing company mounted the printing plate on a press, inked the raised areas, and pulled proofs. These were delivered to Bradley. Using watercolor, he applied color to explore the final placement and design of the red and yellow areas. After selecting an arrangement, Bradley prepared artwork for the red and the yellow printing plates. This artwork was sometimes drawn on translucent vellum paper placed over the master line art. Art for the red printing plate was made by painting a flat shape for the hair area and creating a mottled texture over part of the dress. Artwork for the yellow plate consisted of a large painted shape covering most of the area of the poster. This art would have been prepared with black ink because black photographs better in the camera. Both pieces of artwork were sent to the printer, who made film negatives in the engraver's camera, and then exposed these to two more light-sensitive printing plates.

Painted color swatches were delivered to the printer with the artwork, and the printer mixed inks as closely as possible to the colors Bradley specified.

Printers used steam-powered presses if the press run was long; hand- or foot-pedal powered presses were still used for very short runs. In either case, typical letterpresses of the era printed only one color at a time. The yellow plate was mounted on the press first, and yellow ink was placed in the ink fount. "Make-ready" involved making all the adjustments to the press for the smooth, even printing of ink on paper. The yellow printing was followed by red and blue. Each color was left to dry before the next color was added. In 1895, the available yellow inks posed a serious problem for printers because they dried very slowly. When the second and third colors were printed, the printer had to carefully adjust the registration of the printing plates to ensure an accurate alignment of the three colors of ink printed in sequence on the poster.

Bradley specified transparent inks and used this to good effect in the poster. Where the blue overlaps the flat yellow areas, the colors mix and become green. In some places, red, yellow and blue all overlap, making black. Perhaps the small typography was not over-printed on part of the pressrun, and these posters, without the fine print, may have been sold to collectors.

Proofs were usually delivered to the client and to the designer for their approval; often both would visit the printing firm for press checks while the job was being printed.

After the press run was complete, a poster-hanger would be sent through the streets of Chicago, using a bucket of paste and a stiff brush to affix the posters to walls all across the city. Weathering and overposting of other posters destroyed most of the press run, so only a few copies of many turn-of-the-century posters survive to this day.

Printers and designers then, as now, had a spirit of experimentation and invention, so this poster may not have been produced exactly as described here. Still, this scenario provides one possible version for transforming an artist's visualization into a printed poster at the turn of the century.

Printing Processes and Turn-of-the-Century Posters

Printing is the transfer of ink from a printing surface to a substrate, usually paper. There are four major categories of printing, all of which were used to produce posters at the turn of the century.

Relief Printing is reproduced from a raised surface; an ordinary rubber stamp is typical of this process. There are several kinds of relief printing:

Woodcut printing, the oldest form of printing, was invented in China some time before the 8th century A.D. Early Chinese printers cut away the wood around calligraphy and images drawn on flat blocks of wood to make a raised image. Ink was applied to the raised, cut-out surface of the block, then a sheet of paper was laid over the inked block. Pressure was applied to the back of the paper, either by rubbing or pressing, to transfer the inked image to the paper. Only a few turn-of-the-century posters were printed by using woodcut. **(See cat. no. 53.)**

Letterpress printing, a method of relief printing that was used widely from the 15th century through the 20th century, derives its name from a movable-type process invented by the 15th-century German printer Johann Gutenberg. This process involves printing from the raised surfaces of type, made up of individually cast metal letters, numbers, punctuation marks, and spaces. The individual pieces of type were assembled or "composed" by hand, one line of text at a time, to make up a whole page of text. The type was then locked into a rigid frame and placed or "imposed" on the metal bed of a printing press. As for woodcut printing, ink was applied to the raised surfaces of the type and pressure was applied to transfer the ink to paper. Many turn-of-the-century posters, especially those that were mostly typographic, were reproduced by this method. **(See cat. no. 105.)**

Sometimes woodcuts or photoengraving plates were locked into the printing press with the hand-set type and printed together. In other cases, letterpress was used to add type to an image printed by another process, such as lithography or stencil printing. **(See cat. nos. 35, 49, and 74.)**

Photoengraving is a photomechanical process for making a relief printing plate. The image to be reproduced is photographically transferred by means of a chemical coating on the flat metal surface of a printing plate.

Acid is used to etch away the areas that do not print, leaving a raised image that can be printed on a letterpress. (See cat. nos. 20, 21.)

The halftone process permitted the tones of black-and-white art and photography to be reproduced by printing press. First, a continuous-tone subject, such as a regular photograph, would be photographed through a screen made up of fine horizontal and vertical lines. This would break up the tones of the original photograph, to create an image that appears to be made up of a series of tiny dots. The screen, and the resulting dot pattern, would be small enough to blend into tones in the viewer's eyes. (See cat. no. 106.)

By the turn of the century, full-color illustrations were reproduced by the four-color halftone process. Four halftone negatives were shot from the original artwork using filters to separate the image into red, yellow, blue, and black. A letterpress plate was made for each color. When all four plates were printed one on top of the other using translucent inks, the resulting image would appear to "reassemble" the full range of colors of the original. (See cat. no. 59.)

Intaglio Printing is reproduced from an image that is cut or depressed into a printing surface. We associate it today with engraved wedding invitations, fine stationery, and business cards whose type is raised on the paper. Because intaglio printing does not hold up well for large images or long pressruns, this process was seldom used to print turn-of-the century posters.

Copperplate engravings are produced by scratching a picture, design, or lettering into a smooth, flat sheet of copper. Ink is applied to the surface and forced into the depressions. Any ink remaining on the flat surface is wiped away, then a sheet of damp paper is pressed onto the plate, pulling the ink from the depressions to make the image.

Gravure is the term generally used for contemporary commercial intaglio printing processes.

Planographic Printing is reproduced from a flat surface. Planographic printing processes, generally called lithography, were used to print the vast majority of turn-of-the-century posters.

Lithography means "stone printing" and was so named because the earliest lithographs in the late 1700s were printed from a flat stone surface. Lithography is based on the simple principle that oil and water do not mix. The image is applied to a smooth, flat stone using an oil-based medium, either

a wash or a waxy crayon. The stone is moistened, so that the water saturates the bare surface of the stone but is repelled by the oily image. When an oil-based ink is applied to the stone, it only adheres to the oily surface of the image. (See cat. nos. 85 and 93.)

Chromolithography is color lithographic printing from a series of stones, each with a different ink color. By overprinting as many as 30 colors or more in precise registration, nineteenth-century lithographers were able to make stunning color reproductions. (See cat. no. 101.) By the 1890s, many posters were printed from plates made of aluminum, zinc, or other metals whose surfaces had been treated to make them porous. The images were applied to the metal plates either by hand or by photomechanical methods using an oil-based material. The metal printing plates offered several advantages over stone: they were lighter in weight, could be curved to fit on cylinder printing presses, and made larger posters possible. (See cat. no. 97.)

Offset lithography is a planographic process in which an inked impression is first made on a rubber-blanketed cylinder, then transferred onto the paper. Offset printing was invented in 1904 and was perfected much later; therefore, it was not yet available to print posters at the turn of the century.

Stencil Printing is produced by cutting a design or lettering into a sheet material, then forcing ink through the openings onto the surface to be printed.

Silkscreen printing is the most prevalent form of stencil printing. The stencil is attached to a sheet of fine silk cloth that has been stretched tightly on a wooden frame. Stencil enables printers to produce vibrant areas of brilliant opaque colors and was sometimes used for posters with small press runs.

Resist printing is another form of screen printing. In this case, the stencil is painted onto the areas of the screen where ink is not needed to create the image. In the case of photo-silkscreen, the photographic negative, in the form of a thin film, is adhered to the screen, and the ink is pressed through to create the positive photographic image. ⊠

These Diagrams illustrate the four basic types of printing. They show a cross-section of the printing plate used to print a series of three dots. Imagine that each printing plate has been sawed in half through the middle of the dots.

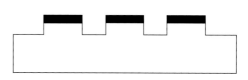

Relief Printing The three dots are raised, and the ink is applied to the raised surfaces.

Intaglio Printing The three dots are cut or incised into the flat surface of the printing plate, then filled with ink.

Planographic Printing The three dots are printed from a flat surface. The dots have been applied with a greasy substance so oil-based ink will adhere to them.

Stencil Printing The three dots are holes in a material that keeps the ink from being pressed through the screen. Ink is forced through these holes onto the surface to be printed.

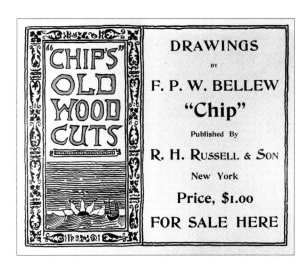

CHAPTER 5
Catalogue of the Collection

1 **"Chip's" Old Wood Cuts**
ca. 1896
Commercial relief and letterpress
25.4 x 31.4 (10 x 12 3/8)
Unsigned
Published by: R. H. Russell & Son, New York
Virginia Museum of Fine Arts Purchase, The Arthur and
Margaret Glasgow Fund and The Sydney and Frances
Lewis Endowment Fund, acc. no. 90.101

TO THE READER:

The posters in this catalogue, all from the collection of the Virginia Museum of Fine Arts, are listed alphabetically by last name of artist.

Poster titles, as listed, include only the most pertinent identifying information printed on the face of the poster.

Dimensions are of the image only, not the entire sheet, and are given first in centimeters, then inches (height by width).

Unless otherwise specified, the signatures given are those that appear on the poster as printed by the same graphic technique used for the rest of the poster. In rare instances an additional signature appears on the poster in pencil or ink, and is so indicated.

When known, the names of both publisher and printer are cited.

ARTIST UNKNOWN

It is very possible that Frank P. W. Bellew (ca. 1860–1894), a cartoonist, designed this poster and his related series of "quaint and amusing sketches . . . consisting of travesties on various topics of the day done after the curious manner of the old wood engraving."[1] Yet even if he is indeed the artist, no biographical information is available regarding his work.

1. From an advertisement printed in *Books and Artistic Publications* (New York: R. H. Russell Publishers, 1899), unpaginated.

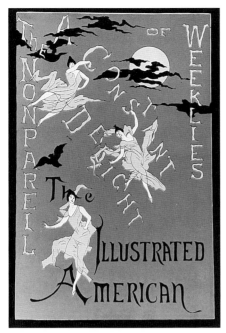

2 **The Illustrated American**
October 1895
Letterpress
40.6 x 27.9 (16 x 11)
Unsigned
Virginia Museum of Fine Arts, Gift of Dr. and Mrs. Robert
Koch, acc. no. 93.23

3 **Picture Posters**
November 1895
Lithograph
37.5 x 25.4 (14 3/4 x 10)
Unsigned
Published by: Macmillan & Co.
Virginia Museum of Fine Arts, Gift of Dr. and Mrs. Robert
Koch, acc. no. 93.24

4 **The Clack Book**
ca. 1896
Lithograph
52.7 x 36.8 (20 3/4 x 14 3/4)
Signed lower right: *F. D. S.*
Printed by: Grand Rapids Lithographing Company
Virginia Museum of Fine Arts Purchase, The Arthur and
Margaret Glasgow Fund and The Sydney and Frances
Lewis Endowment Fund, acc. no. 90.109

ARTIST UNKNOWN

The Illustrated American was founded in
New York in 1890 by Lorillard Spencer. Self-
proclaimed as "The Nonpareil of Weeklies —
A Constant Delight," the publication published four volumes a year from 1890 to
1892 and two volumes yearly until 1900.
The contents included articles on all subjects
as well as news and pictures. Some of the
finest illustrators contributed to the magazine, including Thomas Nast. Color lithographs and a few large woodcuts of "Old
Masters" appeared in early volumes, but most
of the magazine's illustrations were executed
by halftone.

The price was originally twenty-five cents
per number or ten dollars for a year's subscription, a high price that was not afford-
able for many people. The size soon was
reduced to lower the price to ten cents per
copy. In its final stage *Illustrated American*
was "mainly a repository of portraits."[1]

1. Frank Luther Mott, *A History of American
Magazines: 1885-1905* (Cambridge, Mass.: The Belknap
Press of Harvard University Press, 1957), 36.

ARTIST UNKNOWN

Ironically, the artist of this poster for a book
by Charles Hiatt, an art and poster collector
and a noted authority on posters during the
1880s and 1890s, is unidentified. The full
title of the book is *Picture Posters: A Short
History of the Illustrated Placard, with
Many Reproductions of the Most Artistic
Examples in all Countries.* Unfortunately,
none of these "artistic examples" resemble
this poster, presumably executed by an
anonymous illustrator for the Macmillan
Company to advertise the English book (published by George Bell and Sons, London,
1895) in America. In his preface Hiatt credits
Charles Ffoulkes for his "specially drawn"
cover and Henri de Toulouse-Lautrec for the
frontispiece, "a hitherto unpublished study
for a poster."

ARTIST UNKNOWN

The "F. D. S." (initialed in the lower right cor-
ner of this poster) could possibly be Frederic
Dorr Steele (1873-1944), who illustrated
numerous books for New York publishers,
including the Century Company, Charles
Scribner's Sons, R. H. Russell, Doubleday,
and Dodd, Mead & Co.

The Clack Book, "a burlesque on the
popular little magazines of the day," was
produced in Lansing, Michigan.[1] The publication appeared in monthly illustrated
editions from April 1896 to June 1897.

1. Frederick Winthrop Faxon, *Ephemeral Bibelots:
A Bibliography of Modern Chap-Books and Their
Imitators* (Boston: The Boston Book Company, 1903), 10.

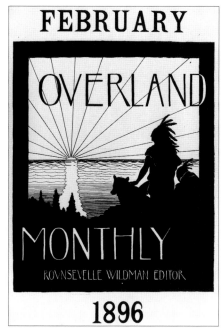

5 **Overland Monthly**
February 1896
Letterpress
40.9 X 27.9 (16 1/8 X 11)
Unsigned
Virginia Museum of Fine Arts Purchase, The Arthur and
Margaret Glasgow Fund and The Sydney and Frances
Lewis Endowment Fund, acc. no. 90.34

6 **The Century for March**
1896
Commercial lithograph
50.8 x 33.0 (20 x 13)
Signed lower right: *E. B. BIRD*
Published by: The Century Co., New York
Printed by: H. A. Thomas & Wylie Lith. Co.,
  New York
Virginia Museum of Fine Arts Purchase, The Arthur and
Margaret Glasgow Fund and The Sydney and Frances
Lewis Endowment Fund, acc. no. 90.33

7 **Outing for April**
1897
Letterpress
46.4 x 30.8 (18 1/4 x 12 1/8)
Signed lower right: *G. W. Bonte*
Published by: J. H. Worman, New York
Virginia Museum of Fine Arts, Gift of Dr. and Mrs. Robert
Koch, acc. no. 93.25

ELISHA BROWN BIRD
1867–1943

E. B. Bird graduated from the Massachusetts
Institute of Technology in 1891, and although
he had studied architecture, he became a
commercial designer and a writer in Boston
and New York. By 1894 he was illustrating
several American periodicals, designing
posters, and writing articles about them.
Bird designed at least sixteen posters
between 1895 and 1897, which he preferred
to have "photomechanically reproduced
[rather than] redrawn by staff technicians."[1]
Bird's 1896 poster for *The Century for
March* received critical acclaim both home
and abroad. He was also among the group of
artists, following Will Bradley, who continued
the series of posters for Stone & Kimball's
The Chap-Book.

Frederic Thoreau Singleton, writing in an
1896 edition of *Poster Lore,* commented that
"Mr. E. B. Bird would ask of a poster that it fill
the following requirements: 'It should have
as few lines as possible to tell the whole
story. As few colors. It should advertise the
merchandise or purpose for which it was
made. It should have carrying points, that is,
be clearly seen at a distance in drawing and
lettering. It should contain a little of the real,
the ideal and the imaginative.'"[2]

1.   David W. Kiehl, *American Posters of the 1890s in The
Metropolitan Museum of Art, including the Leonard A.
Lauder Collection* (New York: The Metropolitan Museum
of Art; distributed by Harry N. Abrams, New York, 1987), 184.
2.   Frederic Thoreau Singleton, *Poster Lore*, bk. 1, pt. 4
(Kansas City, Mo.: The Red-Pale Press, July 1896), 89.

GEORGE WILLARD BONTE
1873–?

Outing magazine was founded in Albany,
New York, by William Bailey Howland. The
magazine was printed in monthly or semian-
nual volumes and underwent many changes
in its thirty-nine years of existence (May
1882 through April 1923). Titles included
Outing, Outing and the Wheelman, and *The
Outing Magazine.* There were seven different editors, and the magazine was published
in three different places—Albany, Boston,
and New York; not surprisingly it suffered
unsteady circulation and profit levels. Under
editors Poultney Bigelow and Caspar Whitney
(1886–1888 and 1900–1909 respectively), the
magazine was considered a distinguished
periodical. One constant element throughout the magazine's existence was its purpose
as a gentleman's outdoor magazine.[1] Biographical information about George Willard Bonte
is unavailable.

1.   Frank Luther Mott, *A History of American
Magazines, 1885-1905* (Cambridge, Mass.: The Belknap
Press of Harvard University Press, 1957), 633–38.

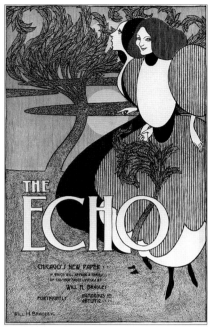

8 **The Chap-Book**
1894
Lithograph
50.5 x 35.5 (19 7/8 x 14)
Signed lower left: *WILL H / BRADLEY /'94*
Published by: Stone & Kimball, Chicago and
Boston
Virginia Museum of Fine Arts Purchase, The Adolph D.
and Wilkins C. Williams Fund, acc. no. 89.64

9 **The Echo**
1894
Letterpress
53.9 x 36.8 (21 1/4 x 14 1/2)
Signed lower left: *Will H. Bradley*
Printed by: The Chicago Photo Engravers Co.
Virginia Museum of Fine Arts Purchase, The Adolph D.
and Wilkins C. Williams Fund, acc. no. 89.65

WILL H. BRADLEY
1868–1962

Will Bradley, who was born in Boston, Mass-achusetts, on July 10, 1868, was the son of a cartoonist for *The Daily Item*, a newspaper published in Lynn, Massachusetts.[1] For the most part, Bradley was a self-taught artist. At the age of twelve he became a "printer's devil" with *The Iron Agitator* in Ishpeming, Michigan, and after four years he signed on as an apprentice in the design department of Rand McNally in Chicago. Later he became a designer with Chicago's Knight & Leonard Printing Company.

At age nineteen Bradley began his career as a freelance illustrator. In 1893 he was commissioned by W. I. Way & Co. to design the cover and decorations for *The Colum-bian Ode* in conjunction with the World's Columbian Exposition. The next year he received his first important commission from Chicago's trade journal, *The Inland Printer*, to design its monthly cover. He eventually designed eighteen covers for that company, from 1894 to 1896. His first poster, "The Twins" was also executed in 1894 for Stone & Kimball's publication *The Chap-Book* (**cat. no. 8**). Evidence of the Art Nouveau style can be seen in most of Bradley's early designs. Although his work has been compared to that of the English artist Aubrey Beardsley,

there is at least one writer who does not view Bradley's work as derivative of Beardsley; instead, he considers the similarities in their styles "cases of parallel development, achiev-ing similar goals in graphic design." This writer further notes the absence of Beardsley's "immoral innuendos" in Bradley's work and the significant influence of William Morris and the English Arts and Crafts Movement.[2] *The Chap-Book, Thanksgiving No.* of 1895 (**cat. no. 14**), with its flowing lines, rhythmic patterns, and contrasting flat color forms, illustrates Bradley's mastery of the Art Nouveau style.

Bradley continued and expanded his own projects throughout the 1890s, leaving Chicago in 1894 and moving to Springfield, Massachusetts, where he established the Wayside Press. The name comes from his belief that he "had always intended to be an artist and considered printing only a wayside to achieving that end," and he chose the dan-delion as its insignia "because the dandelion is a wayside growth."[3] He created his own publication, *Bradley, His Book* (**fig. 1.16**), for which he served as publisher, editor, designer, illustrator, and sometimes writer.

In 1898 Bradley opened an art and design service in New York. At this time his designs

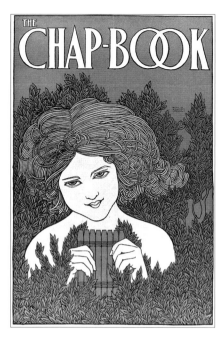

10 **Entertainment for Old and Young**
ca. 1894–95
Letterpress
45.7 x 30.4 (18 x 12)
Signed at right: *Will H. / Bradley*
Virginia Museum of Fine Arts Purchase, The Arthur and
Margaret Glasgow Fund and The Sydney and Frances
Lewis Endowment Fund, acc. no. 90.35

11 **The Chap-Book**
January 1895
Letterpress
53.9 x 36.5 (21 1/4 x 14 3/8)
Signed and dated lower right: *WILL. H. BRADLEY –
1895*
Published by: Stone & Kimball, Chicago and
Boston
Virginia Museum of Fine Arts Purchase, The Arthur and
Margaret Glasgow Fund and The Sydney and Frances
Lewis Endowment Fund, acc. no. 90.38

12 **The Chap-Book**
1895
Letterpress
54.5 x 38.3 (21 1/2 x 15 1/8)
Signed upper right: *WILL H. / BRADLEY*
Published by: Stone & Kimball, Chicago and
Boston
Virginia Museum of Fine Arts Purchase, The Arthur and
Margaret Glasgow Fund and The Sydney and Frances
Lewis Endowment Fund, acc. no. 90.40

WILL H. BRADLEY
Continued

became less heavily decorated to appeal to the mass public, in contrast to the work he had done in Massachusetts, which was more related to the Arts and Crafts Movement.

Throughout his career Bradley was especially interested in the use of typography and its integration into his overall design. According to Edgar Breitenbach, "after the poster craze subsided . . . [Bradley] embarked on a career as a typographer and became one of the best in America."[4] Bradley was active as a designer, art director, and writer well into the twentieth century; he died in 1962 in La Jolla, California.

1. Voluminous writing exists on Will Bradley, including many articles by Dr. Robert Koch, a co-author of this catalogue. An extensive account of this artist's life is provided in Victor Margolin's *The Poster Renaissance*. The catalogue for *Bradley, His Work: An Exhibition* also includes an excellent account of his extraordinary life and artistic career by Bradley himself.
2. David W. Kiehl, *American Posters of the 1890s in The Metropolitan Museum of Art, including the Leonard A. Lauder Collection* (New York: The Metropolitan Museum of Art; distributed by Harry N. Abrams, New York, 1987), 184-85.
3. Victor Margolin, *American Poster Renaissance* (New York: Watson-Guptill, 1975), 25.
4. Edgar Breitenbach, "A Brief History," *The American Poster* (New York: American Federation of Arts, 1967), 17.

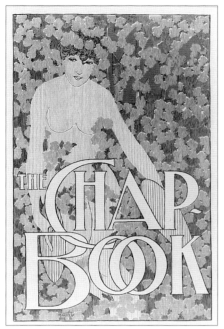

13 The Chap-Book
May 1895
Letterpress
56.2 x 41.2 (22 1/8 x 16 1/4)
Signed lower left: *BRADLEY*
Published by: Stone & Kimball, Chicago and
　Boston
Virginia Museum of Fine Arts Purchase, The Arthur and
Margaret Glasgow Fund and The Sydney and Frances
Lewis Endowment Fund, acc. no. 90.39

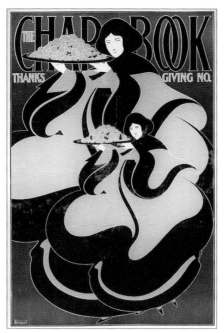

14 The Chap-Book, Thanksgiving No.
1895
Lithograph
50.8 x 34.9 (20 x 13 3/4)
Signed lower left: *WILL.. H / BRADLEY.*
Published by: Stone & Kimball, Chicago and
　Boston
Virginia Museum of Fine Arts Purchase, The Sydney
and Frances Lewis Art Nouveau Fund, acc. no. 74.5.1

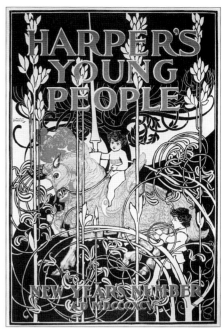

15 Harper's Young People, New Year's
　　Number, 1895
Letterpress
28.8 x 20.6 (11 3/8 x 8 1/8)
Signed center left: *.. WILL. H. / BRADLEY*
Published by: Harper and Brothers, New York
Virginia Museum of Fine Arts Purchase, The Arthur and
Margaret Glasgow Fund and The Sydney and Frances
Lewis Endowment Fund, acc. no. 90.44
*This image, conceived to look like a poster, was
actually an advertisement in a magazine.*

16 Whiting's Ledger Papers
1895
Lithograph
50.5 x 23.5 (19 7/8 x 9 1/4)
Signed upper right: *BRADLEY*
Virginia Museum of Fine Arts Purchase, The Arthur and
Margaret Glasgow Fund and The Sydney and Frances
Lewis Endowment Fund, acc. no. 90.42
*This piece has been identified as a "notebook cover,"
although the Virginia Museum's example appears
also to have served as a poster.*

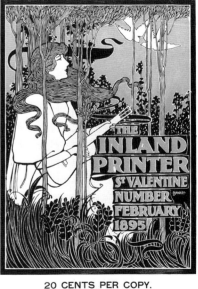

17 The Inland Printer, St. Valentine
　　Number, 1895
Letterpress
50.2 x 36.5 (19 3/4 x 14 3/8)
Signed center left: *Bradley*
Published by: The Inland Printer Company,
　New York
Virginia Museum of Fine Arts Purchase, The Arthur and
Margaret Glasgow Fund and The Sydney and Frances
Lewis Endowment Fund, acc. no. 90.41

18 **The Modern Poster**
1895
Letterpress
49.2 x 29.5 (19 3/8 x 11 5/8)
Signed upper left: *WILL H. BRADLEY 95*; inscribed
lower right in ink: *724* [edition 1000] / *C.S.S.*
Published by: Charles Scribner's Sons, New York
Virginia Museum Purchase, The Glasgow Fund and The
Lewis Endowment Fund, acc. no. 90.36
This poster advertised a book by Arsène Alexander,
M.H. Spielman, H.C. Bunner, and August Jaccaci.

19 **Bradley, His Book**
June 1896
Letterpress
51.2 x 25.7 (20 1/8 x 10 1/8)
Signed lower left: *BRADLEY*
Published by: The Wayside Press, Springfield,
Massachusetts
Virginia Museum of Fine Arts Purchase, The Arthur and
Margaret Glasgow Fund and The Sydney and Frances
Lewis Endowment Fund, acc. no. 90.122

WILL H. BRADLEY
Continued

20 **The Ault & Wiborg Company**
ca. 1900
Letterpress
30.7 x 21.6 (12 1/8 x 8 1/2)
Signed lower right: *BRADLEY*
Published by: Ault & Wiborg Company, Cincinnati
Virginia Museum of Fine Arts Purchase, The Arthur and
Margaret Glasgow Fund and The Sydney and Frances
Lewis Endowment Fund, acc. no. 90.45
This image, conceived to look like a poster, was actu-
ally an advertisement in a promotional booklet.

21 **The American Chap-Book**
September 1904
Letterpress
64.2 x 29.8 (25 1/4 x 11 3/4)
Unsigned
Published by: American Type Founders Co., Jersey
City, New Jersey
Virginia Museum of Fine Arts Purchase, The Arthur and
Margaret Glasgow Fund and The Sydney and Frances
Lewis Endowment Fund, acc. no. 90.43

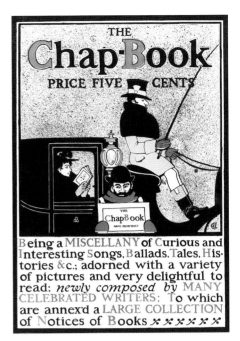

22 **The Chap-Book**
1895
Letterpress
107.3 x 71.1 (42 1/4 x 28)
Signed lower center: *C. F. Bragdon*
Published by: Stone & Kimball, Chicago and
    Boston
Printed by: Stone & Kimball, Chicago
Virginia Museum of Fine Arts Purchase, The Arthur and
Margaret Glasgow Fund and The Sydney and Frances
Lewis Endowment Fund, acc. no. 90.47

23 **The Chap-Book**
1896
Letterpress
46.0 x 32.0 (18 1/8 x 12 5/8)
Signed lower right of image: artist's monogram *CB*
Published by: Stone & Kimball, Chicago and
    Boston
Virginia Museum of Fine Arts Purchase, The Arthur and
Margaret Glasgow Fund and The Sydney and Frances
Lewis Endowment Fund, acc. no. 90.46

CLAUDE FAYETTE BRAGDON
1866–1946

Bragdon was born in Oberlin, Ohio, but attended high school in Oswego, New York, while working part-time with the architect A. J. Hopkins. After graduation in 1884, he worked as a draftsman in Rochester with Charles Ellis, in New York with Bruce Price, and in Buffalo with Von Green and Wicks. During the 1890s Bragdon entered a partnership with Edwin S. Gordon and William H. Orchard and also worked as a designer for Stone & Kimball. In addition to being one of the designers for *The Chap-Book*, Bragdon illustrated books, lettered title pages, and created pictorial bindings for Stone & Kimball.[1]

Bragdon studied architecture in Paris and, while there, collected posters by the leading French designers and became an expert on this art form. Upon returning to the United States, he worked for several years as an illustrator. In 1897 he became a member of the Rochester Arts and Crafts Society and produced catalogue cover designs for their exhibitions. According to his colleague, the architect Harvey Ellis, Bragon was "a guiding spirit" for the group.[2]

Bragdon created posters for *The Chap-Book* and for the *Rochester Post Express*. He also wrote about posters and poster collecting as well as the Arts and Crafts Movement for *Scribner's* and *Life*. Later, he also wrote books, including *The Beautiful Necessity*. Bragdon established the Manas Press in 1909 with the primary purpose of publishing theosophy books.[3] He died in New York City in 1946.

1. Sidney Kramer, *A History of Stone & Kimball and Herbert S. Stone & Co., with a Bibliography of Their Publications, 1893–1905* (Chicago: Norman W. Forgue, 1940), 36, 95.
2. Coy L. Ludwig, *The Arts and Crafts Movement in New York State, 1890s–1920s* (New York: Gallery Association of New York State, 1983), 78.
3. Ibid., 79.

24 **Victor Cycles**
1898
Lithograph
71.1 x 49.2 (28 1/8 x 19 3/8)
Signed lower left: *R. J. Campbell Designer*;
  inscribed across bottom: *Copyright. 1898.*
  by Overman Wheel Co., Chicopee Falls,
  Mass., USA

Virginia Museum of Fine Arts Purchase, The Arthur and
Margaret Glasgow Fund and The Sydney and Frances
Lewis Endowment Fund, acc. no. 90.110

R. J. CAMPBELL
Dates unknown

This poster is one of many illustrating the
growing interest in bicycling near the turn
of the century (see also Will Carqueville,
Duplex Safety Saddle poster, **cat. no. 25**);
there were also articles on the trend in several publications such as *The Wheelman*,
Recreation, and others. With the development of an easily balanced bicycle and the
invention of the pneumatic tire, bicycling
became not only a sport in which the entire
family could engage, but also a symbol of
freedom for the "new woman." In fact, it was
acceptable for even a "proper" lady to cycle.
Campbell created an intriguing three-dimensional image by layering his message, "Ride A
Victor," over swirling black and white ovals
that weave across the elements in the poster.
He provides a startling focal point in the omi-
nous face that peers through the assemblage
above what seems to be a glowing crystal
ball derived from the design of a bicycle
chain. Perhaps Campbell intended to attract
a wide variety of potential Victor Cycle own-
ers by intimating that bicycles would provide
a ride into the future.

25 **The Duplex Safety Saddle**
ca. 1894–95
Lithograph
54.0 x 35.2 (21 1/4 x 13 7/8)
Inscribed lower right: *CARQUEVILLE LITH CO*
  CHICAGO
Printed by: Carqueville Litho Company, Chicago

Virginia Museum of Fine Arts Purchase, The Arthur and
Margaret Glasgow Fund and The Sydney and Frances
Lewis Endowment Fund, acc. no. 90.48

WILL CARQUEVILLE
1871–1946

26 **Lippincott's for January**
1895
Lithograph
48.2 x 32.0 (19 x 12 5/8)
Signed lower right: -*WILL – CARQUEVILLE*-
Published by: J. B. Lippincott Co., Philadelphia
Virginia Museum of Fine Arts Purchase, The Arthur and
Margaret Glasgow Fund and The Sydney and Frances
Lewis Endowment Fund, acc. no. 90.49

27 **Lippincott's April**
1895
Lithograph
48.2 x 31.4 (19 x 12 3/8)
Signed lower right: *Will Carqueville*; inscribed in
image across bottom of magazine cover:
Copyright, 1895, by J. B. Lippincott Company
Published by: J. B. Lippincott Co., Philadelphia
Virginia Museum of Fine Arts Purchase, The Arthur and
Margaret Glasgow Fund and The Sydney and Frances
Lewis Endowment Fund, acc. no. 90.50

28 **International April**
1897
Letterpress
52.3 x 35.5 (20 5/8 x 14)
Signed lower right: *Will Carqueville*
Published by: International, Chicago
Virginia Museum of Fine Arts Purchase, The Arthur and
Margaret Glasgow Fund and The Sydney and Frances
Lewis Endowment Fund, acc. no. 90.51

A native of Chicago and the son of a pioneer in lithography, William L. Carqueville began studying art at age sixteen in the art school of Henry F. Spread.[1] He trained as a lithographer in his father's firm, Shober and Carqueville, which produced theatrical posters. Before going to Paris to continue his art studies around 1896 or 1898, Carqueville was commissioned to design several posters for *Lippincott's* and *International* magazines **(cat. nos. 26, 27, 28)**.[2] As a student at the Colarossi School (affiliated with the Académie Julian) he won the Concors (honors) of the year.[3]

Carqueville returned to Chicago where he established his own lithography workshop and worked for the *Chicago Tribune, International, Poster Advertising Magazine, The Chap-Book,* and *Lippincott's*. Some critics consider Carqueville's illustrations to be reminiscent of Edward Penfield's. However, as one scholar has noted, such criticism is "unnecessary. If anything, Carqueville's posters of 1894–95 more directly acknowledge French contemporaries."[4] Author Charles Hiatt, his contemporary, found Carqueville to have the ability to use color contrasts in a manner unlike those he considered crudely done in England.

Carqueville was also a painter, and in 1921 he won a gold medal at the Art Institute of Chicago.[5] Carqueville was one of only three Chicagoans listed in the *Encyclopedia Britannica* as an "authority on American posters."[6]

1. This information and the subsequent information listed as "Lillis" have been extracted from a letter, dated April 5, 1944, from Carqueville's wife, Mrs. Lillis Carqueville, to Joseph T. Ryerson after she received a catalogue of his "poster exhibit." According to this letter, which is in the archives of the Chicago Historical Society, Henry Spread's art school was located at Clark and Adams Streets.
2. Conflicting dates for the beginning of Carqueville's study in Paris exist: David Kiehl's poster catalogue lists 1896 as the date, while Lillis Carqueville said he went to Paris in "about 1898."
3. Lillis.
4. David W. Kiehl, *American Posters of the 1890s in The Metropolitan Museum of Art, including the Leonard A. Lauder Collection* (New York: The Metropolitan Museum of Art; distributed by Harry N. Abrams, New York, 1987), 185.
5. Lillis Carqueville's letter states that Carqueville won a gold medal at the "Art Institute" (probably the Art Institute of Chicago) with Deforest Shook and J. Wellington Reynolds [sic]. The 1921 date was derived from the Wellington Jarard Reynolds entry in *Who Was Who in American Art*, ed. Peter Hastings Falk (Boston: Sound View Press, 1985), 514.
6. Lillis.

29 **Pan-American Exposition**
1901
Lithograph
121.9 x 64.1 (48 x 25 1/4)
Inscribed lower left: *Gies & Co., Buffalo, N.Y., U.S.A.*
Published by: Gies & Company, Buffalo, New York
Virginia Museum of Fine Arts Purchase, The Arthur and
Margaret Glasgow Fund and The Sydney and Frances
Lewis Endowment Fund, acc. no. 90.111

EVELYN RUMSEY CARY
1855–1924

The daughter of Bronson C. Rumsey, a prominent member of the Buffalo aristocracy and one of the founders of the Buffalo Fine Arts Academy,[1] Evelyn Rumsey was born in Buffalo and lived in the Rumsey family home all her life.[2] After marrying Dr. Charles Cary, she continued to participate in and support the Buffalo artistic community, studying at the Buffalo Art Students League with Alfred Quinton Collins around 1888[3] and exhibiting work with the Buffalo Society of Artists from its inception in 1891. She also took part in annual exhibitions held at the Buffalo Fine Arts Academy.

While serving on the Board of Women Managers for Buffalo's Great International Fair of 1901, Cary executed a painting (now in the collection of the Buffalo and Erie County Historical Society) for the Pan-American Exposition. This painting became the basis for a poster (**cat. no. 29**) that was chosen as a signature image for the Exposition, and its publication firmly established her reputation. According to *Profitable Advertising*, a contemporary trade magazine, "no similar enterprise had ever been so well publicized [as the Pan-American Exposition]. Evelyn Rumsey Cary's 'Spirit of Niagara' was one of the sixty-seven printed items issued by the Pan-American Publicity Bureau."[4] Gies & Company of Buffalo printed 120,962 copies of the nine-color lithograph.[5]

The painting, inspired by the exposition site, includes an allegorical figure, Niagara's legendary "Maid of the Mist," enveloped in the falls. The poster's lettering and stylized laurel leaf were chosen by Frederick Flager Helmer to incorporate Cary's use of Art Nouveau techniques.[6] K. Porter Aichele noted that this poster would have been especially appealing to the "sophisticated elite" who responded to the then-current trend of stylish posters. "There seems to be little doubt that the 'Spirit of Niagara' was chosen by the organizers of the exposition because Cary's painted illusion effectively advertised the product.... The 'Spirit of Niagara' was designed to attract a broad spectrum of the American public. Cary's image made the romance of Niagara a vivid reality to anyone for whom a trip to Niagara was the dream of a lifetime."[7]

1. Susan Krane, William H. Gerdts, and Helen Raye, *The Wayward Muse: A Historical Survey of Painting in Buffalo* (Buffalo, New York: Albright-Knox Art Gallery, 1987), 44-45.
2. Obituary in the *Buffalo Evening Times*, April 21, 1924, 1. Evelyn Rumsey Cary's lifelong home was located at the intersection of Delaware and Tracy Streets.
3. Chris Petteys, *International Dictionary of Women Artists: An International Dictionary of Women Artists Born before 1900* (Boston: G. K. Hall & Co., 1985), 126.
4. K. Porter Aichele, "'The Spirit of Niagara': Success or Failure?" *Art Journal*, vol. 44, no. 1 (Spring 1984): 46.
5. Ibid.
6. Ibid. Helmer, a commercial artist, was hired to commission advertising and to supervise the production of all publications associated with the Exposition.
7. Aichele, 49.

30 **The Philistine**
December 1895
Letterpress
53.3 x 35.6 (21 x 14)
Signed lower left with artist's monogram: *C*
Published by: Elbert Hubbard, East Aurora,
    New York
Virginia Museum of Fine Arts, Gift of Dr. and Mrs. Robert
Koch, acc. no. 93.26

DWIGHT RIPLEY COLLIN
Dates unknown

The Philistine was a so-called little magazine published by Elbert Hubbard's Roycroft Press. Subtitled *A Periodical of Protest*, it served as a vehicle for advertisements, as well as providing Hubbard with opportunities for proclaiming his views on just about all aspects of life. Hubbard, "a popular writer as well as a master of self-promotion," established his press in East Aurora, a suburb of Buffalo, New York, in 1895.[1] After visiting England and allegedly meeting William Morris, Hubbard assembled a community of skilled craftsmen.

The major graphic designers for Roycroft Press were William Wallace Denslow, Samuel Warner, and Dard Hunter. For many years Roycroft printed some of the most highly regarded books in this country, but the quality began to deteriorate when Hunter left Roycroft in 1909. After Hubbard and his wife, Alice, died in the sinking of the Lusitania in 1915, publication of *The Philis-*tine was discontinued, but the Roycroft community continued under the leadership of his son. The Roycroft Press, according to Jean-François Vilain,

> printed some of the most exciting books of the time along with some poor ones. And, thanks to Elbert Hubbard's genius for advertising, Roycroft efforts spawned an awareness of fine printing in a large public which, otherwise, would have stayed unaware of it.
>
> Morris' influence through the Kelmscott books, and indirectly, through the works of Hubbard . . . and the literary presses, inspired many young artists and designers who welcomed the idea that a book could be beautiful and express the personality of its makers.[2]

Although Hubbard commissioned Collin to design this striking and enigmatic poster, no biographical information is known about the artist. *The Philistine* was one of the most successful of the little magazines of the period, reaching a circulation of 125,000 at one point.[3] Volume 2, Number 1 of *The Philistine* advertised Collin's poster on the back cover: "Mr. Collin's PHILISTINE poster will be sent, securely packed, to any address upon receipt of 25 cents by the publishers. It is sufficiently artistic, both in drawing and in color to deserve a place among the few really remarkable posters of the year. Fifty copies, printed by hand on Japan Vellum, numbered and signed by Mr. Collin, are offered for sale at $1 each. *Very few remain*."[4]

1. Jean-François Vilain, "Printing and American Arts and Crafts, 1890–1910," *Arts and Crafts Quarterly*, vol. 3, no. 3 (September 1990): 27.
2. Ibid., 28-29.
3. Frank Luther Mott, *A History of American Magazines: 1885–1905* (Cambridge, Mass.: The Belknap Press of Harvard University Press, 1957), 646.
4. *The Philistine*, vol. 2, no. 1 (December 1895), back cover.

31 **Pioneer Poster Makers of the West**
November 1896
Letterpress
27.9 x 17.8 (11 x 7)
Signed lower right: *William Denslow*
Published by: The Chicago Photo Engraving Co.
Virginia Museum of Fine Arts, Gift of Dr. and Mrs. Robert
Koch, acc. no. 93.28

32 **The Home Magazine**
August 1898
Letterpress
33.0 x 22.9 (13 x 9)
Signed lower left: *DENSLOW*/ seahorse motif
Virginia Museum of Fine Arts, Gift of Dr. and Mrs. Robert
Koch, acc. no. 93.27

WILLIAM WALLACE DENSLOW
1856–1915

Born May 5, 1865, in Philadelphia, W. W. Denslow began his formal art training in New York at the age of fourteen, studying first at the Cooper Institute for the Advancement of Science and Art and then at the National Academy of Design. He also studied at what was eventually called the Salmagundi Club.[1]

During the late 1870s to early 1880s, Denslow designed posters and show cards for the theater and consequently obtained commissions for the New York weekly magazine *The Theatre*. The publishers of the *Herald* in Chicago offered him a full-time position as a designer. He spent a good part of his career in Chicago, although he frequently took jobs in other areas, including Denver and San Francisco. His brief stay in California acquainted him with Oriental art, which later influenced his graphic design.[2]

Denslow's illustrations for the Columbian Exposition of 1893 gained him a reputation as a freelance illustrator. Robert Koch described Denslow's style around 1896 as "both broadly humorous and boldly Art Nouveau. His ability to caricature is compa-

rable only to that of his better-known English contemporary, Max Beerbohm."[3]

In 1896 he joined Elbert Hubbard's Roycroft Shops in East Aurora, New York, where he designed a number of fine books and created the monthly cartoons for the back covers of Hubbard's *The Philistine*, as well as posters for that so-called little magazine. Denslow had become Hubbard's favorite designer by 1900, when "it was generally agreed that the most beautiful books ever produced in the United States were being turned out" by the Roycroft Press.[4]

His best-remembered and most familiar illustrations, however, are those he did at the turn of the century for Frank L. Baum's *The Wonderful Wizard of Oz*. This experience gave him a unique opportunity to illustrate a children's book while working directly with the author in creating a world of fantasy.

In 1903 he married for a third time and purchased a mansion on an island in Bermuda, crowning himself "King Denslow I."[5] His later work was not deemed suitable for the more advanced methods of graphic technology such as photo reproduction. In addi-

tion, librarians shunned his books; Anne Carroll Moore, organizer of the children's division of New York Public Library, was quoted as saying: "Such books as Denslow's *Mother Goose,* with a score of others of the comic poster order, should be banished from the sight of impressionable young children."[6] Forced to give up his Bermuda home, he moved back to New York where he died in 1915 "alone and depressed. . . . Not even an obituary appeared in the newspapers for which he had worked so many years."[7]

1. Susan E. Meyer, *A Treasury of the Great Children's Book Illustrators* (New York: Abradale Press, Harry N. Abrams, 1987).
2. Ibid., 259.
3. Robert Koch, "Elbert Hubbard's Roycrofters as Artist-Craftsmen," *Winterthur Portfolio 3* (Winterthur, Delaware: Henry Francis du Pont Winterthur Museum, 1967), 171.
4. Ibid.
5. Meyer, 264.
6. Ibid., 265.
7. Ibid.

33 **Modern Art**
1895
Lithograph
53.9 x 38.6 (21 1/4 x 15 1/4)
Signed lower left: *Arthur W Dow*
Published by: Louis Prang & Co., Boston
Virginia Museum of Fine Arts Purchase, The Adolph D.
and Wilkins C. Williams Fund, acc. no. 89.66.

34 **The Lotos**
February 1896
Lithograph
38.6 x 26.0 (15 1/4 x 10 1/4)
Unsigned
Published by: The Cycle Publishing Co., New York
Virginia Museum of Fine Arts Purchase, The Arthur and
Margaret Glasgow Fund and The Sydney and Frances
Lewis Endowment Fund, acc. no. 90.52

35 **The Lotos**
March 1896
Lithograph and letterpress
55.9 x 35.6 (22 x 14)
Signed lower left: *A W DOW* in circle
Published by: The Cycle Publishing Co., New York
Virginia Museum of Fine Arts, Gift of Dr. and Mrs. Robert
Koch, acc. no. 93.29

ARTHUR WESLEY DOW
1857–1922

Born in Ipswich, Massachusetts, Dow studied art in Paris, but perhaps the greatest artistic influence was his friendship with Ernest F. Fenollosa, Curator of Oriental Art of the Museum of Fine Arts, Boston. It was Fenollosa who introduced him to Japanese art through that museum's collections, and Dow embraced the concepts of Japanese art as the guiding force in the creation of his paintings, prints, and posters. Dow felt that he could combine the best of Eastern and Western art to form a synthesis and apply it to his subjects. He combined line, mass, and color to structure his works, using a careful building process to create beauty through simplicity.

Dow is known to have created only a few posters, the most important of which was produced in 1895 for *Modern Art* (**cat. no. 33**), an important artistic journal published by Louis Prang & Co.[1] This poster shows clearly how Dow applied his principles of design to the lithographic medium. The simplification of the landscape (based on the Ipswich River) to almost abstract elements, the natural subtle gradations of color, and the geometric placement of natural forms against

a border of lotus blossoms all owe a debt to Japanese design concepts.[2] Dow also produced posters to advertise *The Lotos*, Fenollosa's New York-based magazine.

Dow became a noted art instructor, teaching at Pratt Institute (1894–95) and the Art Students League (1897–1903). He also taught Oriental art at Columbia Teachers College. Among his most renowned students was Georgia O'Keeffe.

The example of the *Modern Art* poster in the Virginia Museum's collection is especially important in that it is a printer's proof with larger margins than usual. The printer's hatch marks used to register the various colors are still evident along the edge.

1. For an account of the important work of the printer Louis Prang, see Katharine Morrison McClinton, *The Chromolithographs of Louis Prang* (New York: Clarkson N. Potter, 1973).
2. According to Ernst and Johanna Lehner, *Folklore and Symbolism of Flowers, Plants, and Trees* (New York: Tudor Publishing Company, 1960), 120, the lotus, a flower that Dow used repeatedly in his illustrations, symbolizes "mystery and truth, . . . perfection and purity, . . . past, present, and future."

36 **Harper's Magazine, Christmas**
1898
Lithograph
40.9 x 28.6 (16 1/2 x 11 1/4)
Signed lower left: *HARVEY ELLIS*
Published by: Harper and Brothers, New York
Virginia Museum of Fine Arts Purchase, The Arthur and
Margaret Glasgow Fund and The Sydney and Frances
Lewis Endowment Fund, acc. no. 90.113

HARVEY ELLIS
1852-1904

Architect, designer, and artist Harvey Ellis was the eldest son of a minor politician in Rochester, New York.[1] After being expelled from West Point in January 1872, Ellis spent the following year studying with Edwin White at the National Academy of Design and later worked as an apprentice architect.

In 1879 Ellis and his brother established the architecture firm of Harvey & Charles S. Ellis in Rochester, and in 1884 Harvey helped organize the Rochester Arts and Crafts Society with Claude F. Bragdon and M. Louis Stowell. He spent the following years working for various architectural firms in Utica, St. Louis, and St. Paul, eventually returning to Rochester where he became more active with the local art circles, joining the Rochester Art Club and the Vagabond Club.[2]

Around 1893 lack of architectural commissions allowed Ellis to return to painting.[3] May Bragdon, the sister of artist Claude Bragdon and a member of Ellis's social circle, indicates in a diary entry dated October 18, 1897, that Ellis was beginning a familiar pattern of distancing himself from friends and had started drinking again, despite the fact that he suffered from kidney disease.[4] His paintings began to show the influence of the Japanese style and often contained religious imagery, as does this particular poster created in 1898. In 1903 Gustav Stickley, the most prominent force in the American Arts and Crafts Movement, hired Ellis with the hope of attracting a different, more affluent clientele to purchase his furniture. Ellis worked for Stickley for less than a year before he died at age fifty-two. Because of the brevity

of his employment with Stickley's Craftsman Workshops, Ellis-designed furniture is considered very rare. A number of pieces are in the collection of the Virginia Museum of Fine Arts **(see fig. 1.22A)**.

One of Ellis's colleagues, M. Louis Stowell, wrote in the September 1910 issue of *Palette and Bench* that an intriguing aspect of Ellis's work "occurred when the man allowed full expression of his mystic side and gave us a remarkable series of pictures significant of deep religious feeling."[5]

1. Marie Via, "Beloved Vagabond: The Paintings and Drawings of Harvey Ellis," *Arts & Crafts Quarterly* (1st Quarter 1991): 26-32.
2. Ibid., 29.
3. Ibid.
4. Ibid.
5. Ibid.

37 **February Scribner's**
1899
Letterpress
50.8 x 37.8 (20 x 14 7/8)
Signed lower center: *C. D. Gibson*; inscribed:
    *Copyright 1899 Charles Scribner's Sons,
    New York*
Printed by: The Grignard Litho. Co., New York
Virginia Museum of Fine Arts Purchase, The Arthur and
Margaret Glasgow Fund and The Sydney and Frances
Lewis Endowment Fund, acc. no. 90.53

38 **The Christmas Scribner's**
1899
Lithograph
55.9 x 36.8 (22 x 14 1/2)
Signed below image in ink: *C. D. Gibson*; inscribed
    lower left: *Copyrighted 1899 / Charles Scribner's
    Sons, N.Y.*; inscribed lower right: *H. G. '99*
Published by: Charles Scribner's Sons, New York
Virginia Museum of Fine Arts Purchase, The Arthur and
Margaret Glasgow Fund and The Sydney and Frances
Lewis Endowment Fund, acc. no. 90.54

CHARLES DANA GIBSON
1867–1944

Probably one of the best known and most popular of all poster designers, Charles Dana Gibson was born in Roxbury, Massachusetts, and died in New York City. Gibson studied briefly with the sculptor Augustus St. Gaudens and, from 1884 to 1885, at the Art Students League in New York. He then worked as a staff artist for *Life* magazine, and later created his famous "Gibson Girl," widely believed to be based on his wife, the lovely Irene Langhorne.[1]

Gibson's skillful black-and-white illustrations depicting fine-featured members of the upper classes assured his success and popularity. His work—both illustrations and drawings—was in great demand. He supplied illustrations for *Scribner's*, *Harper's*, *The Century*, and London's *Pall Mall* magazine. (Gibson's posters were not executed by him but were adapted from his black-and-white drawings by staff artists.[2]) Collections of his magazine illustrations were published under titles such as *The American Girl Abroad, Drawings—Humorous American Painters, Pictures of People, People of Dickens*, and *The Education of Mr. Pipp of New York*.

1. Gibson married Miss Langhorne in St. Paul's Episcopal Church in Richmond, Virginia, in November 1895, an event considered to have been the highlight of the city's social season. See Virginius Dabney, *Richmond: The Story of a City* (Charlottesville, Virginia: The University Press of Virginia, 1990), 263.
2. David W. Kiehl, *American Art Posters of the 1890s in The Metropolitan Museum of Art, including the Leonard A. Lauder Collection* (New York: The Metropolitan Museum of Art; distributed by Harry N. Abrams, New York, 1987), 187.

39 **Pearson's**
May, ca. 1899
Lithograph
46.9 x 30.8 (18 1/2 x 12 1/8)
Signed lower right in image area: *L. Goodfellow*
Virginia Museum of Fine Arts, Gift of Dr. and Mrs. Robert
Koch, acc. no. 93.30

40 **Lippincott's, January**
1896
Letterpress
32.1 x 20.8 (12 5/8 x 8 3/16)
Signed lower right: *J. J. Gould, Jr.*
Published by: J. B. Lippincott Co., Philadelphia
Virginia Museum of Fine Arts, Gift of Dr. and Mrs. Robert
Koch, acc. no. 93.31

41 **Lippincott's, June**
1896
Lithograph
34.8 x 22.8 (13 11/16 x 9)
Signed lower left in image area: *J. J. Gould Jr.;*
    inscribed lower left: *COPYRIGHT 1896 BY
    J.B. LIPPINCOTT. CO.*
Published by: J. B. Lippincott Co., Philadelphia
Virginia Museum of Fine Arts, Gift of Dr. and Mrs. Robert
Koch, acc. no. 93.32

L. GOODFELLOW
Dates unknown

Pearson's was originally an English magazine
that began an American edition in 1899.[1]
Many English periodicals were transported to
America where they often thrived. Although
no biographical information is known about
L. Goodfellow, he obviously intended to
emphasize the cost of the magazine, since 8¢
is the dominant graphic motif set against a
stylized landscape. Since so many so-called
little magazines were being published, competition was stiff and price was important.

1. Frank Luther Mott, *A History of American Magazines,
1885-1905* (Cambridge, Mass.: The Belknap Press of
Harvard University Press, 1957), 228.

JOSEPH J. GOULD, JR.
ca. 1875–ca. 1935

Although little is known of J. J. Gould's biography, he was evidently "one of the best
known poster designers of his time."[1] After
studying at the Pennsylvania Academy of the
Fine Arts, he worked as an artist, primarily
in Philadelphia.

From 1895 to 1897 Gould worked for J. B.
Lippincott Company and eventually took
over Will Carqueville's position as poster
designer for the company's series of monthly
magazines. In 1896 he created twelve distinct designs, one for each edition of the
publication.[2] Two other posters that Gould
designed for Lippincott are known, one for
the "Select Novel" series, and the other for
Marie Corelli's popular fiction.[3] In addition
to his work for *Lippincott's* magazine, Gould
also illustrated several Philadelphia journals
and later designed posters and covers for *The
Saturday Evening Post.*

Gould's posters have been compared to
those of Penfield and Carqueville. Author
and critic Charles Hiatt, one of Gould's contemporaries, referred specifically to the
February, July, and November issues of
Lippincott's as bearing a "distinct general
likeness to the productions of Mr. Penfield"
and added that "the color schemes of both
these artists are simple and brilliant without

a suspicion of that rawness which comes
of the unskillful contrast of large masses of
primary colours. . . ."[4]

Hiatt commented critically on Gould's
use of realistic representation in his work
for *Lippincott's* but remarked, "for this he
should not be blamed, for doubtless the
publishers insist on it. As I noted last
month, Mr. Maxfield Parrish and Mr. Will
Carqueville seem to have suffered from the
same futile obligation."[5]

Other critics have defended Gould's originality. As David Kiehl pointed out, "His compositions lacked the static frontal quality of
Penfield's figures, implied greater movement
through diagonal composition, and relied on
planes of nonprimary color."[6]

1. Carolyn Keay, *American Posters of the Turn of the
Century* (New York: St. Martin's Press, 1975), 29.
2. Charles Hiatt, "Pictorial Book Advertisements in
America," as quoted in Keay, 24-25.
3. David W. Kiehl, *American Art Posters of the 1890s in
The Metropolitan Museum of Art, including the Leonard
A. Lauder Collection* (New York: The Metropolitan
Museum of Art; distributed by Harry N. Abrams, New York,
1987), 187.
4. Hiatt as quoted in Keay, 24.
5. Ibid.
6. Kiehl, 187.

42 **Dr. Jameson's Raiders**
1896
Letterpress
25.4 x 38.7 (10 x 15 1/4)
Signed lower left: *ERNEST / HASKELL / 96*;
   inscribed upper left: *Dec / 96*
Published by: R. H. Russell & Son, New York
Virginia Museum of Fine Arts, Gift of Dr. and Mrs. Robert
Koch, acc. no. 93.33

ERNEST HASKELL
1876-1925

Born in Woodstock, Connecticut, Ernest Haskell was a painter, lithographer, etcher, and writer who earned praise both during his lifetime and after his death. Childe Hassam, the renowned painter and etcher, said of the younger artist: "I think of his etchings as among the best that have been made—absolutely and wholly personal, some so meticulously and highly finished that it may be said that they were really in the spirit of the old masters."[1]

In a very flattering 1948 catalogue essay about Haskell, John Taylor Arms wrote that he "possessed in full measure those qualities which set an artist apart from his fellows and mark his oeuvre with the seal of permanence. With an emotional intensity that permeated the man's whole being and life, his response to it was alike controlled by a disciplined intellectuality and yet given complete and untrammeled expression by a consummate mastery of his craft attained by a lifetime of experiment, study, and indefatigable practice."[2]

According to another writer, Haskell followed two prevailing styles in his posters: "one tended to flat areas of color and idealized subjects . . . closely akin to the work of Edward Penfield and Will Carqueville [and J. J. Gould]; the other was filled with a *joie de vivre* that owed much to Jules Chéret and the French school."[3] *Dr. Jameson's Raiders*, the book by Richard Harding Davis for which Haskell designed this poster, was an account of a dramatic but failed British raid, led by Sir Leander Starr Jameson, into the Transvaal region during the Boer Wars. In his poster designs, Haskell was undoubtedly influenced by the French school, having studied in Paris for several years before returning to the United States to paint and to create illustrations and prints.

On November 1, 1925, after visiting New York to arrange for a exhibition of watercolors he had just completed in California, Haskell was killed in an automobile accident while returning to his home in Maine.[4]

1. *Commemorative Exhibition, Ernest Haskell (1876-1925)*, February 2-28 (New York: Galleries of Kennedy & Company, 1948), 5.
2. Ibid., 3.
3. Kiehl, 188.
4. Peter Hastings Falk, ed., *Who Was Who in American Art* (Boston: Sound View Press, 1985), 267. Conflicting locations of Haskell's fatal car accident exist: either in Bath or Phippsburg, Maine. All sources, however, agree that he was involved in an accident.

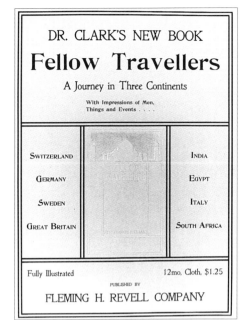

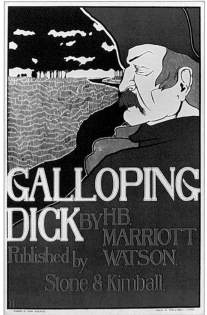

43 **The Chap-Book**
April 1896
Lithograph
52.1 x 36.2 (20 1/2 x 14 1/4)
Inscribed lower left: *DESIGNED BY FRANK
   HAZENPLUG*; signed lower left center: *FH*,
   the artist's conjoined initials
Published by: Stone & Kimball, Chicago
Printed by: Stone & Kimball, Chicago
Virginia Museum of Fine Arts Purchase, The Arthur and
Margaret Glasgow Fund and The Sydney and Frances
Lewis Endowment Fund, acc. no. 90.56

44 **Fellow Travellers**
ca. 1896
Book by the Rev. Francis E. Clark
Letterpress and embossing
40.8 x 38.1 (20 x 15)
Unsigned
Published by: Fleming H. Revell Company
Virginia Museum of Fine Arts Purchase, The Arthur and
Margaret Glasgow Fund and The Sydney and Frances
Lewis Endowment Fund, acc. no. 90.57

45 **Galloping Dick**
1896
Book by H. B. Marriott Watson
Lithograph
53.9 x 36.1 (21 1/4 x 14 1/4)
Inscribed lower left: *DESIGNED BY FRANK
   HAZENPLUG* under the artist's cypher, *FH*
Published by: Stone & Kimball, Chicago
Printed by: Stone & Kimball, Chicago
Virginia Museum of Fine Arts Purchase, The Glasgow Fund
and The Lewis Endowment Fund, acc. no. 90.55

FRANK HAZENPLUG
1873–after 1911

Frank Hazenplug was born in Dixon, Illinois, and studied art informally in Chicago. His first professional work in the art world came in 1894, when he was hired by publishers Stone & Kimball and later Herbert S. Stone & Company.[1] Hazenplug worked with Will Bradley and eventually succeeded him as artist for Stone & Kimball when Bradley moved to Springfield, Illinois. While working for Stone & Kimball, Hazenplug created posters, illustrated short stories and books, and also designed book bindings.

Hazenplug's other graphic work includes illustrations for eight books published by Way & Williams,[2] at least one poster for Emerson and Fisher ("the Cincinnati carriage brothers"),[3] and designs for *Living Posters*.[4]

Garrison Garfield Rhodes, whose article on Hazenplug appeared in *The Chap-Book* in 1896, described his style as constantly changing:

> One month saw him drawing like the most decadent Englishmen; the next saw him imitating the style of old woodcuts; and the third found him attacking the problems of poster-making which have been mastered only by the French. He was teaching himself and his chosen method was imitation, deliberate,

earnest, and constant. . . . He finally ceased to be an imitator. If he has learned from others how to draw he has not learned what to draw. Passing all his life in this unlovely city of Chicago, living little with books, and less with bookish people, he has had little inspiration from the outside.[5]

Around 1896, the year he executed the poster for *Galloping Dick* (**cat. no. 45**), he may have shortened his name to "Frank Hazen."[6] In the April 1, 1896 issue of *The Chap-Book*, Stone & Kimball advertised the publication of *Galloping Dick* as "being chapters from the Life and Fortunes of Richard Ryder, sometime Gentleman of the Road." They also quoted some critics of the book: "In these times of smothery, erotic novels and unhealthy wailings, a dashing book of this nature is a blessing *(Chicago News)*."[7] The binding of the book bears a portrait of a "gentleman of the road" but does not resemble Hazenplug's dramatic poster image. No credit has been given in the book to the artist of the binding.

Nothing is known of Hazenplug after 1911.

1.   Rolf Achilles, "*The Chap-Book* and Posters of Stone & Kimball at the Newberry Library," *The Journal of Decorative & Propaganda Art, 1875–1945*, no. 14 (Fall 1989): 76.
2.   Letter from Rozanne Barry, Research Assistant, School of Librarianship, Berkeley, California, to Margaret Scriven, Librarian, Chicago Historical Society, January 25, 1962.
3.   Victor Margolin, *American Poster Renaissance* (New York: Watson-Guptill, 1975), 215.
4.   Carolyn Keay, *American Posters of the Turn of the Century* (New York: St. Martin's Press, 1975), 29.
5.   Harrison Garfield Rhodes, "Frank Hazenplug: A Little Boy among the New Masters," *Chap-Book*, vol. 4, no. 9 (March 15, 1896): 412.
6.   Barry letter to Scriven. In her letter Ms. Barry also wrote that Hazenplug is sometimes listed as "Hasenplug."
7.   "Advertisements," *The Chap-Book*, vol. 4, no. 10 (April 1, 1896): xi.

46 **Robert Blum's Great Decorative Painting in January Scribner's,** 1895
Letterpress
43.8 x 31.8 (17 1/4 x 11 7/8)
Signed lower right: *SK* in circle
Published by: Charles Scribner's Sons, New York
Printed by: J. E. Rhodes, New York
Virginia Museum of Fine Arts, Gift of Dr. and Mrs. Robert Koch, acc. no. 93.34

47 **October Century**
1895
Letterpress
47.6 x 30.3 (18 3/4 x 11 7/8)
Signed lower left with artist's conjoined initials
Published by: The Century Co., New York
Virginia Museum of Fine Arts Purchase, The Arthur and Margaret Glasgow Fund and The Sydney and Frances Lewis Endowment Fund, acc. no. 90.60

WILLIAM SERGEANT KENDALL
1869-1938

Born in Spuyten Duyvil, New York, William Sergeant Kendall studied in Philadelphia with Thomas Eakins before working at the Art Students League in New York. Kendall later went to Paris, where he studied at the Académie Julian and then at the Ecole des Beaux Arts, exhibiting at the school's Salon of 1890. He exhibited frequently both in the U.S. and abroad, and won numerous awards until his death in 1938.

Kendall executed three posters for *Scribner's.* These posters are unique in that they are portraits, drawn from life, of three well-known artists: Charles Dana Gibson (August 1895), Robert Blum (January 1896), and Charles Stanley Reinhart (1896).[1]

The artist portrayed in the Virginia Museum's poster, Robert Blum (1857–1903), was a highly successful artist whose work was influenced by the art of Japan. In 1890, Blum was commissioned by *Scribner's* to provide illustrations for a series of articles on Japan. As a result, Blum created a number of works in pencil, pastel, and watercolor, as well as wood engravings and etchings. He also completed a few oil paintings, one of which, *The Temple Court of Fudo Sama at Meguro, Tokyo,* 1891, is in the collection of the Virginia Museum **(see fig. 1.24A, p.22).**

Kendall portrays Blum in a relaxed and casual attitude with no attributes of his profession. It is an informal portrait of a standing figure, though not necessarily that of an artist; and the man looks as though he would feel right at home in the late twentieth century. In addition to the inquisitive nature of Kendall's posters, their appearance is also unique in that he skillfully lettered the posters himself, replacing the conventional *Scribner's* masthead.[2]

From 1913 to 1922 Kendall served as Dean of the School of Fine Arts at Yale University, and is listed as living in Hot Springs, Virginia, in 1929.[3]

1. Will M. Clemens, *The Poster,* vol. 1, no. 1 (January 1896), unpaginated.
2. David W. Kiehl, *American Art Posters of the 1890s in The Metropolitan Museum of Art, including the Leonard A. Lauder Collection* (New York: The Metropolitan Museum of Art; distributed by Harry N. Abrams, New York, 1987), 188.
3. Peter Hastings Falk, ed., *Who Was Who in American Art* (Boston: Sound View Press, 1985), 332.

HERBERT MYRON LAWRENCE
1852-1937

No biographical information is available for this artist before 1895, when he apparently was employed in *The Century's* art department, designing at least four advertising posters for books and magazine placards.[1]

The striking colors and strong outlines of Lawrence's poster design have an obvious connection to the Arts and Crafts Movement and especially to the design of ceramic tiles of the period. The image is a bold statement of a full-rigged sailboat, its speed emphasized by the stylized waves and cloud patterns. It is interesting to note the tension that Lawrence creates by having the sail and the bow break the border, which in all other instances contains the image.

1. Roberta Waddell Wong, *American Posters of the Nineties* (Boston: Boston Public Library, 1974), 36.

48 **The Inland Printer, November**
1896
Lithograph
27.6 x 20.6 (10 7/8 x 8 1/8)
Signed lower right on stone: *J. C. Leyendecker*
Published by: The Inland Printer Company,
    Chicago and New York
Virginia Museum of Fine Arts, Gift of Dr. and Mrs. Robert
Koch, acc. no. 93.35

49 **August Now Ready**
The Inland Printer, 1897
Letterpress and lithograph
43.2 x 26.0 (17 x 10 1/4)
Signed lower right: *J. C. Leyendecker '97*
Published by: The Inland Printer Company,
    Chicago and New York
Virginia Museum of Fine Arts Purchase, The Arthur and
Margaret Glasgow Fund and The Sydney and Frances
Lewis Endowment Fund, acc. no. 90.58

JOSEPH CHRISTIAN LEYENDECKER
1874–1951

In the acknowledgments of his 1974 monograph on Leyendecker, Michael Schau noted that there was very little written material on the artist, "one of America's most popular illustrators during the first half of this century," and that "the sensibility, style, and technique of the man must be found in his pictures—in the posters, illustrations, advertisements and hundreds of magazine covers. Verbal confirmation of Leyendecker's sensitivity, elegance, vitality, and pride of craftsmanship is not necessary; the pictures say it all."[1]

J. C. Leyendecker was born in Germany in 1874, but his family emigrated to America in 1882 and settled in Chicago, where in 1890 he began as an unpaid apprentice in the Chicago engraving house of J. Manz & Co.[2] While learning the engraving business he also attended night classes at the Chicago Art Institute.

Early in 1896 Leyendecker won *The Century* cover contest with a design closely aligned to the Art Nouveau style. Maxfield Parrish, already well-established in the field, won second prize **(see cat. no. 62)**.

Leyendecker and his brother Frank left for Paris in September 1896 for two years, studying at the Académie Julian and at the Colarossi School. At this time the Académie was led by Adolphe William Bouguereau, who considered the study of the classics essential and taught his students the goal of excellence in making exact copies.

Even before returning to Chicago in September 1897, Leyendecker received several commissions as a result of *The Century* contest, including twelve monthly designs for covers and posters from the editors of *The Inland Printer,* to be published from January through December 1897.[3]

Leyendecker also contributed posters and magazine covers for some of the most highly recognized publications in America, including *Scribner's, Interior Design,* and *The Chap-Book*; and he created covers for *Collier's* from 1898 to 1918. The first of approximately 322 *Saturday Evening Post* covers was done in 1899.[4] Among the most famous of these images was the annual New Year's baby, which actually originated as a cherub in 1906 and later evolved into a symbol of the holiday.

As an illustrator Leyendecker also created advertisements for many products, some still recognizable today, including Arrow shirt collars, Chesterfield cigarettes, Ivory soap, and Kellogg's Corn Flakes. Perhaps his best known and best remembered designs were his advertisements for the Arrow shirt, from 1905 to 1930.

1. Michael Schau, *J. C. Leyendecker* (New York: Watson-Guptill, 1974), acknowledgements, unpaginated.
2. Walt and Roger Reed, *The Illustrator in America, 1880-1980:A Century of Illustration* (New York: Madison Square Press, 1984), 98.
3. David W. Kiehl, *American Art Posters of the 1890s in The Metropolitan Museum of Art, including the Leonard A. Lauder Collection* (New York: The Metropolitan Museum of Art; distributed by Harry N. Abrams, New York, 1987), 189.
4. Schau, 23.

50 **Familiar Flowers of Field and Garden**
ca. 1895
Lithograph and letterpress
49.8 x 34.6 (19 5/8 x 13 5/8)
Inscribed lower left: *Lincoln. N.Y.*
Published by D. Appleton & Co., New York
Virginia Museum of Fine Arts Purchase, The Arthur and
Margaret Glasgow Fund and The Sydney and Frances
Lewis Endowment Fund, acc. no. 90.61

51 **Now Ready/The Inland Printer**
May 1898
Commercial relief process
43.2 x 26.0 (17 x 10 1/4)
Signed in image, lower center: *J. L. Loveday/98*
Published by: The Inland Printer Company,
    Chicago and New York
Printed by: Osgood Art Colortype Co., Chicago
Virginia Museum of Fine Arts Purchase, The Arthur and
Margaret Glasgow Fund and The Sydney and Frances
Lewis Endowment Fund, acc. no. 90.62

A. W. B. LINCOLN
Dates unknown

Little is known about this artist except for
the fact that he (or she) appears to have
been relatively prolific, having created a
number of designs for posters and book
cover illustrations for publisher Frederick A.
Stokes Company of New York. The artist created at least twenty-one posters advertising
books for that company and may have been
a member of its art department.[1]

   In this case, the artist has used a relatively
conservative representation of flowers and
leaves to depict the theme of the book by
F. Schuyler Mathews. The typography, however, is more avant-garde and eye-catching.
The binding of the book itself utilizes the
exact same design.

1.   David W. Kiehl, *American Art Posters of the 1890s in
The Metropolitan Museum of Art, including the Leonard
A. Lauder Collection* (New York: The Metropolitan Museum
of Art; distributed by Harry N. Abrams, 1987), 189.

J. L. LOVEDAY
Dates unknown

The Inland Printer was one of the leading
print journals of the period, priding itself on
its design, paper, and production. Many of
the leading designers of the day contributed
to the production of the magazine, including
the advertising related to it.

   Unfortunately, nothing has been recorded
about J. L. Loveday, but the artist was obviously significantly influenced by the Art
Nouveau style of the Czechoslovakian artist
Alphonse Mucha. In fact, the profile image
on this poster is very close to those that
Mucha created not only in his lithographs
but also in his rare works of sculpture, such
as the bust *La Nature* in the collection of the
Virginia Museum of Fine Arts.

   Full color has been used in the production of this poster, as was the case in many
of the illustrations in *The Inland Printer*.
Though dependent on European prototypes,
the stock is slick and the colors are vivid,
making it a striking image.

52 **Scribner's Fiction Number**
1895
Lithograph
49.5 x 33.6 (19 1/2 x 13 1/4)
Signed lower left in image area: *Will H. Low;*
    lower right in pencil: *Will H. Low*
Published by: Charles Scribner's Sons, New York
Virginia Museum of Fine Arts Purchase, The Arthur and
Margaret Glasgow Fund and The Sydney and Frances
Lewis Endowment Fund, acc. no. 90.59

WILL HICOK LOW
1853–1932

As evidenced in this remarkable poster, Will Low was greatly influenced by the French academicians. It is interesting to note, however, that during an earlier period he was influenced to a similar degree by the Realists of the Barbizon School, especially Jean Millet. Thus his work tends to reflect the dichotomy of the two rival or warring factions of French art of the late nineteenth century.

Born in Albany, New York, Low studied in Paris at the Ecole des Beaux Arts. This early training is evident in his reliance on classical motifs and his emphasis on the realistic, yet romantic, portrayal of the human figure.

Low was commissioned to illustrate numerous periodicals as well as write articles for them. In this poster, the complex printing of twelve colors has been accomplished by hand-separation, a tour de force on the part of both printer and artist.

In addition to his allegorical paintings, Low is best remembered for his illustrations of Keats's poems as well as for his murals, which he completed for such prominent buildings as the Waldorf-Astoria Hotel. As a muralist, Low won numerous gold medals for his works, including those shown at the Paris Exposition of 1889 and the Columbian Exposition in Chicago in 1893.

Although his work received critical acclaim, this particular poster was not held in high regard by the authors of *The Red Letter,* a so-called little magazine devoted to the study and collection of posters. In its August 1896 issue, the editors commented: "Through the kind permission of Messrs. Chas. Scribner's Sons, we are able to present a small reproduction of their August poster by Will H. Low. It is a most magnificent affair, being reproduced in twelve colors, but has unfortunately, in its composition, far more of the pictorial than the poster spirit. The coloring is beautiful, the drawing excellent, but the details are too evident, its carrying power inferior, and it reminds one, sad to say, of those exquisite picture cards that Prang gives us at Christmas."[1]

1. "The Poster and Decorative Work," *The Red Letter*
(August 1896), unpaginated.

53 **What is That Mother? The Lark My Child, for August,** 1895
Woodcut on Chinese bamboo paper
51.7 x 35.5 (20 3/8 x 14)
Signed lower left: *FL*
Published by: William Doxey, San Francisco
Virginia Museum of Fine Arts Purchase, The Arthur and Margaret Glasgow Fund and The Sydney and Frances Lewis Endowment Fund, acc. no. 90.63

FLORENCE LUNDBORG
1871–1949

Born in San Francisco, Florence Lundborg was a painter as well as an illustrator of books, magazines, and posters. She studied art in Italy, France, and San Francisco, where her teachers were Arthur F. and Lucia Mathews, founders of The Furniture Shop after the great San Francisco fire of 1906. Lundborg's work was especially influenced by Arthur Mathews, who was a painter, while his wife, Lucia, was responsible for decorating, painting, and carving the furniture and other objects that their shop produced.

Lundborg is perhaps best known for her contributions to the short-lived little magazine *The Lark*, published by William Doxey and edited by Gelett Burgess. For just two years, this charming, witty, and irreverent magazine published the writings of Burgess, Jack London, Frank Norris, Arnold Genthe, Upton Sinclair, and others who formed a unique group reflecting the literary aesthetics of the California style. It is perhaps best remembered for Burgess's short, nonsensical poems, such as *The Purple Cow*, which appeared in the first issue of *The Lark*:
"I never saw a purple cow, I never hope to see one; but I can tell you anyhow, I'd rather see than be one."

Lundborg produced posters, such as this one, as well as illustrations for the periodical. She preferred woodblock designs, feeling that they had "more personality of their inventor than the mechanically produced lithograph [could] possibly have."[1] Normally she herself cut the blocks, but in this case she entrusted that responsibility to Burgess. The block was then printed on "a very interesting Bamboo fibre paper used [as] wrapping paper in the Chinese drug stores in San Francisco."[2]

The relative simplicity of the woodcut, the woman's medieval style of dress, and the artist's hand-lettering all combine to form an interesting example of the West Coast Arts and Crafts Movement.

1. Charles Hiatt, "Pictorial Book Advertisements in America," as quoted in Carolyn Keay, *American Posters of the Turn of the Century* (New York: St. Martin's Press, 1975), 25.
2. "The Poster," vol. 1, no. 4 (April 1896): 49, as noted in David W. Kiehl, *American Art Posters of the 1890s in The Metropolitan Museum of Art, including the Leonard A. Lauder Collection* (New York: The Metropolitan Museum of Art; distributed by Harry N. Abrams, New York, 1987), 133.

54 **The Adventures of Captain Horn**
1895
Letterpress and lithograph
41.3 x 30.5 (16 1/4 x 12)
Signed upper right: *BMcM*
Published by: Charles Scribner's Sons, Publishers,
New York
Virginia Museum of Fine Arts Purchase, The Arthur and
Margaret Glasgow Fund and The Sydney and Frances
Lewis Endowment Fund, acc. no. 90.64

55 **The True Mother Goose**
1895
Letterpress
52.7 x 36.5 (20 3/4 x 14 3/8)
Signed left center: *BMcM*; inscribed lower right:
*copyright 1895 by Lamson Wolffe & Co.,
Boston, U.S.A.*
Published by: Lamson Wolffe & Co., Boston
Printed by: Heliotype Printing Co., Boston
Virginia Museum of Fine Arts Purchase, The Arthur and
Margaret Glasgow Fund and The Sydney and Frances
Lewis Endowment Fund, acc. no. 90.65

BLANCHE McMANUS
1870–after 1929

Born in East Feliciana, Louisiana, Blanche McManus studied in London and Paris before returning to America in 1893 and settling in Chicago.

Most of McManus's work consists of magazine and book illustrations, but she also executed at least eight posters, including *The Adventures of Captain Horn,* to promote a book by Frank R. Stockton (**cat. no. 54**), and *The True Mother Goose* (**cat. no. 55**), to promote her own book, which eventually became a children's classic.

She and her husband, Francis Miltoun Mansfield, collaborated to create deluxe travel books, including *The American Woman Abroad* and *Our French Cousins.*[2] The *American Woman Abroad* was described as a "How-to book for American women traveling and living in Europe from the point of view of a practical-minded, middle-class American artist."[3]

Although she was very well known in England, little was written about her in America. She was considered to be "one of those artists whose talent is equalled only by her modesty, who, enamoured of her art and aiming at a patient, painstaking realization of her ideal, has been content to work on in silence. In the estimation of art connoisseurs, Blanche McManus is an artist of unquestionable talent and varied composition, who has already done much striking work. Her execution in the various branches has attracted international attention."[4]

In designing the embossed book cover and end papers for *The True Mother Goose,* which she wrote and illustrated, McManus employed variations on the design of flying and overlapping geese that appear on the poster, thus creating a unified design.

1. David W. Kiehl, *American Art Posters of the 1890s in The Metropolitan Museum of Art, including the Leonard A. Lauder Collection* (New York: The Metropolitan Museum of Art; distributed by Harry N. Abrams, 1987), 189.
2. Chris Petteys, *Dictionary of Women Artists: An International Dictionary of Women Artists Born before 1900* (Boston: G. K. Hall & Co., 1895), 465.
3. Carolyn Keay, *American Posters of the Turn of the Century* (New York: St. Martin's Press, 1975), 29.
4. Clara Erskine Clement, *Women in the Fine Arts: From the Seventh Century B.C. to the Twentieth Century A.D.* (Boston and New York: Houghton, Mifflin, 1904), 236–37.

56 **Kate Carnegie**
ca. 1896
Letterpress
44.4 x 30.5 (17 1/2 x 12)
Signed lower right: *A. C. MORSE*
Published by: Dodd, Mead and Company,
New York
Virginia Museum of Fine Arts Purchase, The Arthur and
Margaret Glasgow Fund and The Sydney and Frances
Lewis Endowment Fund, acc. no. 90.114

57 **Posters in Miniature**
1896
Letterpress
20.0 x 28.9 (7 7/8 x 11 3/8)
Signed lower left: *NANKIVELL/'96*
Published by: R. H. Russell & Son, New York
Virginia Museum of Fine Arts, Gift of Dr. and Mrs. Robert
Koch, acc. no. 93.36

ALICE CORDELIA MORSE
1862–?

A designer of stained glass and book covers as well as posters, Alice Morse was also a painter and bookbinder. Although we have little information about her career, we do know that she was born in Hammondsville, Jefferson County, Ohio; that she studied at New York's Cooper Union school under John La Farge, and later with Louis C. Tiffany & Co.; and that she was active in Brooklyn, New York.

In 1880 the fourth prize for a Louis Prang & Co. Christmas card contest (amounting to $200) was awarded to "Alice S. Morse," perhaps the same artist. Alice Cordelia Morse often exhibited her work, both at the 1893 Chicago Columbian Exposition and annually at the New York Architectural League.

In addition to her 1895 poster for the book *Kate Carnegie* by Ian MacLaren **(cat. no. 56)**, she designed a poster for another Dodd, Mead and Co. publication, *The Paying Guest* by George Gissing.[1]

1. Ruth Malhotra and Christina Thon, *Das frühe Plakat in Europa und den USA*, vol. 1: *Grossbritannien und Vereinigte Staaten von Nordamerika* (Berlin: Gebr. Mann, 1973), 77.

FRANK ARTHUR NANKIVELL
1869–1959

A native of Australia, Frank Arthur Nankivell studied in Japan from 1891 to 1894 before working and studying in San Francisco from 1894 to 1896. His drawings appeared in *The Call*, a San Francisco paper, and in *The Echo*, founded by Percival Pollard in Chicago. In addition, Nankivell himself published a magazine called *Chic*.

In 1896 Nankivell moved to New York, where he served on the staff of *Puck* while creating designs on commission for such publications as *The Clack Book, The Echo*, and the *New York Journal.*

Nankivell's design for *Posters in Miniature* served as both promotional poster and book jacket for the actual book written by his friend Percival Pollard and the artist Edward Penfield. At the time, Pollard was considered to be one of the foremost authorities on and proponents of poster design, publication, and collecting. In the introduction to the book, Penfield wrote: "Within the past few years the word Poster has been growing in significance, until now we look upon it as describing a decoration, thoroughly fin de siècle, and perhaps pleasing. A poster should tell its story at once—a design that needs study is not a poster, no matter how well it is executed. . . . A poster, to be effective, must have the same qualities that a good painting possesses—color, simplicity and composition—but that must be expressed in a different manner. . . . Some of the best examples of the work of masters of the poster-art in France, England, Germany, and America are present, and to them are added numerous designs by men of more or less ability."[1]

It is interesting to note that although R. H. Russell & Son commissioned Nankivell to create the poster and book jacket for *Posters in Miniature*, his work is neither mentioned nor illustrated in the body of the book.

1. Edward Penfield, "Introduction," *Posters in Miniature* (New York: R. H. Russell & Son, 1896), unpaginated.

58 **A Puritan's Wife**
1895
Lithograph
48.2 x 31.7 (19 x 12 1/2)
Signed lower right: *V. OAKLEY*
Published by: Dodd, Mead & Co., New York
Virginia Museum of Fine Arts Purchase, The Arthur and
Margaret Glasgow Fund and The Sydney and Frances
Lewis Endowment Fund, acc. no. 90.66.

59 **The Christmas Century**
December 1902
Letterpress (four-color process)
53.3 x 35.6 (21 x 14)
Signed in medallion, lower right: *V. OAKLEY*;
    inscribed across bottom of image: *Copyright
    1902 by The Century Co.*
Published by: The Century Co., New York
Printed by: American Colortype Co., New York
Virginia Museum of Fine Arts Purchase, The Arthur and
Margaret Glasgow Fund and The Sydney and Frances
Lewis Endowment Fund, acc. no. 90.67

60 **The June Bookman**
1902
Lithograph and letterpress
55.8 x 40.6 (22 x 16)
Signed lower center: *G. C. PARKER*
Virginia Museum of Fine Arts Purchase, The Arthur and
Margaret Glasgow Fund and The Sydney and Frances
Lewis Endowment Fund, acc. no. 90.68

VIOLET OAKLEY
1874–1961

Growing up in New Jersey surrounded by a family of artists, Violet Oakley "liked to say she had been born with a paintbrush in her mouth." In circumstances such as these, "she received encouragement in her ambition to be an artist, unlike so many female artists of the period."[1]

Oakley began her extensive art studies at the Art Students League in New York around 1892 and later enrolled at the Académie Montparnasse after her family moved to Europe. She continued her studies in Philadelphia with Cecilia Beaux, Joseph DeCamp, and Henry Thouron. Toward the end of 1896, she joined Howard Pyle's class at Drexel Institute, having already designed at least one poster for a book by Max Pemberton by this date (**cat. no. 58**).

Oakley's period of study with Pyle was most influential; as one writer said, "no matter how far she traveled, she never left Philadelphia in spirit again, and in many ways remained Pyle's pupil all her life."[2]

For the next decade she illustrated publications such as *McClure's, Collier's Weekly, The Century* (**cat. no. 59**), *Harper's, Everybody's,* and *Ladies' Home Journal.* Although she aspired to become a great artist who would create major paintings and other more tradi-

tional art forms, she supported herself with illustration commissions during this period.

Pyle encouraged her to work and arranged for her to paint two large murals and design a mosaic and five stained-glass windows for the All Angels' Church in New York City, all of which she completed by 1898.[3] Although this was a significant achievement, her most important commission—the "biggest commission ever awarded an American woman artist"[4]—was in 1893, when she painted murals in the Pennsylvania State Capitol in Harrisburg.

Oakley lived and worked in the Philadelphia area with artists Elizabeth Shippen Green and Jessie Willcox Smith in a type of artist's co-op. They later moved into a house that served not only as a studio and home, but also as a gathering-place for local artists. Oakley taught at the Pennsylvania Academy of the Fine Arts from 1912 to 1917, the only female instructor other than Cecilia Beaux.

1. Mahonri Sharp Young, "Violet Oakley: A Message for the World," *American Art & Antiques* (July/August 1978): 51.
2. Ibid.
3. Ibid., 53.
4. Ibid., 51.

Attributed to **G. CUSHMAN PARKER**
1881–?

The "G. C. Parker" whose name appears on this poster is probably Cushman Parker, an illustrator born in Boston, Massachusetts. Parker studied in Boston and designed covers for the *Saturday Evening Post, McCall's,* and *Collier's Weekly.* Shortly after the turn of the century, he worked for George H. Doran Co., New York, publisher of *The Bookman.* The poster for the June 1902 issue of that periodical (**cat. no. 60**) is further evidence that G. C. Parker, as signed, is G. Cushman Parker.

Parker later became a member of the Society of Illustrators and the Artists Guild of the Authors' League of America, New York.

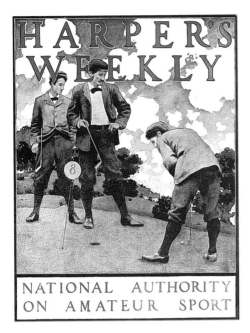

61 **Harper's Weekly**
1896
Photographic lithograph
46.7 x 35.5 (18 3/4 x 14)
Signed left center, inside image: *M.P.*
Published by: Harper and Brothers, New York
Virginia Museum of Fine Arts Purchase, The Arthur and
Margaret Glasgow Fund and The Sydney and Frances
Lewis Endowment Fund, acc. no. 90.80

62 **The Century Midsummer Holiday Number,** August 1897
Lithograph
50.5 x 33.9 (19 7/8 x 13 3/8)
Signed lower right: *Maxfield Parrish*; inscribed
    bottom center: *SECOND PRIZE, CENTURY
    POSTER CONTEST.*
Published by: The Century Co., New York
Printed by: The Thomas & Wylie Lithographic Co.
Virginia Museum of Fine Arts Purchase, The Adolph D. and
Wilkins C. Williams Fund, acc. no. 89.67

63 **Scribner's Fiction Number**
August, 1897
Lithograph
50.4 x 36.8 (19 7/8 x 14 1/2)
Signed lower right: *Maxfield / Parrish / 1897*
Published by: Charles Scribner's Sons, New York
Virginia Museum of Fine Arts Purchase, The Arthur and
Margaret Glasgow Fund and The Sydney and Frances
Lewis Endowment Fund, acc. no. 90.81

MAXFIELD PARRISH
1870-1966

Maxfield Parrish was perhaps one of the most popular and prolific artists of the late nineteenth and early twentieth century. Reproductions of his paintings seemed to adorn every middle-class living and dining room, and his designs for calendars, posters, magazines, and other advertisements could be seen everywhere.

The son of painter and etcher Stephen Parrish, Maxfield Parrish was born in Philadelphia and studied at Haverford College and at the Pennsylvania Academy of the Fine Arts. Having trained briefly with the noted Brandywine Valley artist-illustrator

Howard Pyle, Parrish developed a unique style that combined much of the precision of the academic painters with the simplification of forms derived from Pyle and other leading "modern" artists of the period. Parrish's images were often derived from mythology and legend, with figures set in incredibly beautiful landscapes that could only exist in a dream (**cat. no. 63**). This idyllic imagery permitted the workers in a depressed economy to escape visually to exotic, although imaginary, lands and thus may account for his incredible popularity.

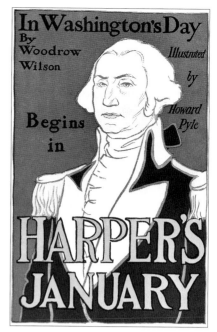

64 **Harper's Bazar, Midsummer Number,** July 1894
Letterpress
33.7 x 23.7 (13 1/4 x 9 5/16)
Signed lower left: *EDWARD PENFIELD*
Published by: Harper and Brothers, New York
Virginia Museum of Fine Arts, Gift of Dr. and Mrs. Robert Koch, acc. no. 93.37

65 **Harper's January**
1896
Lithograph
44.1 x 28.5 (17 3/8 x 11 1/4)
Unsigned
Published by: Harper and Brothers, New York
Virginia Museum of Fine Arts Purchase, The Arthur and Margaret Glasgow Fund and The Sydney and Frances Lewis Endowment Fund, acc. no. 90.70

EDWARD PENFIELD
1866–1925

Edward Penfield, "one of the first artists to work" in the field of poster design, was born in New York.[1] After studying fine arts at the Art Students League, he began working for *Harper's* in 1881. Ten years later, in 1891, he became their art director, and from 1893 to 1898, with few exceptions, he designed the magazine's monthly posters. It was Penfield who initiated the practice of incorporating in his posters the image of a figure holding or reading the magazine being advertised, but he eventually discarded this device when other illustrators began to imitate him.

Penfield's posters have the immediacy that he preached in his introduction to the book *Posters in Miniature* (**see cat. no. 57**). This philosophy, which is based on his knowledge of the work of his French colleagues in their directness and use of color, and the simplification of forms practiced by Japanese printmakers, is at the core of all of Penfield's images. To accomplish his bold designs, he used an enormous range of printing techniques, often making it difficult to identify the processes he used.

Will Bradley, a great admirer of the artist, wrote glowingly about Penfield's January 1895 poster and the textures and richness that he had achieved through technical

processes: "[The] methods of reproduction ... are new, no one else has accomplished so much; no one else has even attempted it. It is not within the scope of this article to tell how all this is effected, and yet the preparation of one color upon charcoal paper, and another color in spatter work and crayon upon another kind of paper, the hammering of a stipple in the metal plate, are all matters worthy of thought."[2]

The subjects of Penfield's posters for *Harper's*—usually members of the leisured and well-bred class relaxing and reading the magazine—were particularly American and were undoubtedly intended to appeal to that same monied class from which they were drawn. These images were an early step toward modern advertising methods. Other Penfield posters, for example the portrait of George Washington he designed for the January 1896 issue of *Harper's* (**cat. no. 65**), used such obvious and familiar imagery that everyone would be attracted to them.

During the 1890s Penfield also designed commercial posters for manufacturers of bicycles, dynamite, and other products, as well as at least fifteen books published by Harper and Brothers, including *Three Gringos in Central America and Venezuela,*

On Snow Shoes to Barren Grounds, and *The Martian* (**cat. no. 72**).[3] In the case of *The Martian,* the same design was used for both the poster and the embossed and gilded book cover, although the text of the book was illustrated by the author, George du Maurier.

1. Carolyn Keay, *American Posters of the Turn of the Century* (New York: St. Martin's Press, 1975), 30.
2. Will Bradley, "Edward Penfield, Artist," *Bradley, His Book,* vol. 1, no. 1 (May 1896), unpaginated.
3. David W. Kiehl, *American Art Posters of the 1890s in The Metropolitan Museum of Art, including the Leonard A. Lauder Collection* (New York: The Metropolitan Museum of Art; distributed by Harry N. Abrams, 1987), 217.

66 **Harper's June**
1896
Lithograph
47.6 x 35.2 (18 3/4 x 13 7/8)
Signed upper left: *Edward Penfield*
Published by: Harper and Brothers, New York
Virginia Museum of Fine Arts Purchase, The Arthur and
Margaret Glasgow Fund and The Sydney and Frances
Lewis Endowment Fund, acc. no. 90.74

67 **Harper's September**
1896
Lithograph
34.9 x 46.3 (13 3/4 x 18 1/4)
Inscribed lower right: artist's bull's-head logo
Published by: Harper and Brothers, New York
Virginia Museum of Fine Arts Purchase, The Arthur and
Margaret Glasgow Fund and The Sydney and Frances
Lewis Endowment Fund, acc. no. 90.69

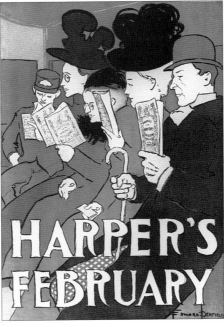

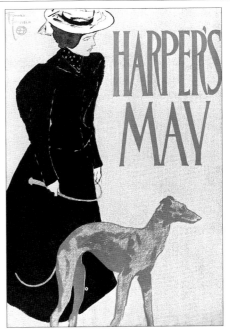

68 **Harper's November**
1896
Lithograph
44.9 x 33.9 (17 11/16 x 13 3/8)
Signed upper right: artist's bull's-head logo,
 EDWARD/PENFIELD
Published by: Harper and Brothers, New York
Virginia Museum of Fine Arts Purchase, The Adolph D. and
Wilkins C. Williams Fund, acc. no. 74.10

69 **Harper's February**
1897
Lithograph
48.9 x 35.8 (19 1/4 x 14 1/8)
Signed lower right: *EDWARD PENFIELD*
Published by: Harper and Brothers, New York
Virginia Museum of Fine Arts Purchase, The Arthur and
Margaret Glasgow Fund and The Sydney and Frances
Lewis Endowment Fund, acc. no. 90.73

70 **Harper's May**
1897
Lithograph and letterpress
47.1 x 33.7 (18 7/16 x 13 1/4)
Signed upper left: *EDWARD/PENFIELD/*
 bull's-head logo
Published by: Harper and Brothers, New York
Virginia Museum of Fine Arts, Gift of Dr. and Mrs. Robert
Koch, acc. no. 93.38

71 **Harper's June**
1897
Lithograph
36.4 x 47.5 (14 5/16 x 18 11/16)
Signed lower right: *EDWARD PENFIELD*
Published by: Harper and Brothers, New York
Virginia Museum of Fine Arts, Gift of Dr. and Mrs. Robert
Koch, acc. no. 93.39

EDWARD PENFIELD
Continued

72 **The Martian**
1897
Lithograph
51.7 x 33.0 (20 3/8 x 13)
Unsigned
Published by: Harper and Brothers, New York
Virginia Museum of Fine Arts Purchase, The Arthur and
Margaret Glasgow Fund and The Sydney and Frances
Lewis Endowment Fund, acc. no. 90.71

73 **Greater New York Number of
Harper's Weekly,** 1897
Lithograph and letterpress
35.5 x 34.9 (14 x 13 3/4)
Unsigned
Published by: Harper and Brothers, New York
Virginia Museum of Fine Arts Purchase, The Arthur and
Margaret Glasgow Fund and The Sydney and Frances
Lewis Endowment Fund, acc. no. 90.72

74 **Poster Calendar**
1897
Lithograph and letterpress
4 sheets, each 35.5 x 25.7 (14 x 10 1/8)
January/February/March signed lower left:
   EDWARD/PENFIELD
April/May/June signed lower right:
   EDWARD/PENFIELD
July/August/September signed lower left:
   EDWARD/PENFIELD
October/November/December signed middle right:
   artist's bull's-head logo/ *EDWARD/PENFIELD*
Published by: R.H. Russell & Son, New York

Virginia Museum of Fine Arts Purchase, The Arthur and Margaret Glasgow Fund and The Sydney and Frances Lewis Endowment Fund, acc. no. 90.75.1/4

75 **Harper's January**
1898
Lithograph and letterpress
47.3 x 35.5 (18 5/8 x 14)
Signed lower center: artist's bull's-head logo
Published by: Harper and Brothers, New York
Virginia Museum of Fine Arts Purchase, The Arthur and
Margaret Glasgow Fund and The Sydney and Frances
Lewis Endowment Fund, acc. no. 90.76

76 **Harper's June**
1899
Lithograph
26.3 x 33.0 (10 3/8 x 13)
Unsigned
Published by: Harper and Brothers, New York
Virginia Museum of Fine Arts Purchase, The Arthur and
Margaret Glasgow Fund and The Sydney and Frances
Lewis Endowment Fund, acc. no. 90.77

EDWARD PENFIELD
Continued

77 **Collier's X'mas**
1903
Lithograph
49.5 x 31.1 (19 1/2 x 12 1/4)
Signed lower right: artist's bull's-head logo
Published by: Collier's, New York
Virginia Museum of Fine Arts Purchase, The Arthur and
Margaret Glasgow Fund and The Sydney and Frances
Lewis Endowment Fund, acc. no. 90.78

78 **The July Number, The Century**
1896
Lithograph (aluminum plate)
51.0 x 35.7 (20 1/16 x 14 1/16)
Inscribed lower left: *E P/ Designed by EDWARD
     POTTHAST*; inscribed lower right: *Printed
     from Aluminum by W. B. Orcutt Company, N.Y.*
Published by: The Century Co., New York
Printed by: W. B. Orcutt Company, New York
Virginia Museum of Fine Arts, Gift of Dr. and Mrs. Robert
Koch, acc. no. 93.40

EDWARD HENRY POTTHAST
1857–1927

Few details are recorded about the life of the American Impressionist artist Edward Henry Potthast, in part because of his "characteristic shyness" and in part because of "the inherent conservatism of his art."[1] Born in Cincinnati, Potthast began his formal art training at the McMicken School of Design, where he is listed as a student in 1870. In addition, attending classes under Thomas S. Noble and Frank Duveneck helped to prepare Potthast for an apprenticeship with Ehrogott Krebs, Co., Lithographers. In 1873, at the early age of sixteen, he was listed in the Cincinnati City Directory as "Eddie Potthast, litho[grapher]."[2] Potthast was offered employment by Strobridge Litho Co. in 1879, and at some point he designed at least one poster, showing a girl balancing on the back of a horse, to advertise the Barnum and Bailey Circus. In 1881, Potthast changed his occupational listing in the City Directory to "artist."[3]

Potthast left for Europe, probably in the fall of 1882, to study in Antwerp and then in Munich before returning to Cincinnati and resuming work with the Strobridge firm. From 1885 to 1887 he was enrolled in evening life classes at the Cincinnati Museum Association Art School (also known as the Academy of Cincinnati), where he again studied with Thomas S. Noble. He later returned to Europe and stayed primarily in France where, through the guidance of American-born Robert W. Vonnoh, he was especially influenced by the French Impressionists. This influence is readily apparent in the seashore paintings for which he is best known, which are like snapshots in their *plein-air* atmosphere and spontaneity of execution.

Upon his return to Cincinnati, Potthast continued his work as a freelance lithographer, eventually moving to New York. He received commissions from *Scribner's* and *Century* magazines, and an 1896 design, after receiving an honorable mention in *The Century* poster contest, was used immediately as the magazine's July poster, in which a lady reads the magazine in the foreground while the artists sketches in the far background (**cat. no. 78**).

1. Arlene Jacobowitz, *Edward Henry Potthast: 1857–1927* (New York: Chapellier Galleries, 1969), unpaginated.
2. Ibid.
3. Ibid.

79 **M'lle New York**
1895
Letterpress
43.2 x 30.5 (17 x 12)
Unsigned
Virginia Museum of Fine Arts, Gift of Dr. and Mrs. Robert
Koch, acc. no. 93.41

T. E. POWERS
Died 1939

No biographical information is available
for this artist, except that he (or she) lived
in Norwalk, Connecticut, and died on
August 14, 1939.[1]

Powers has created a powerful and evoca-
tive image through the use of intense black
and stark white, which is used in areas created by the glow of the candle held by the
woman as she reads a newspaper. Her bare
feet, arm, and shoulder create a rather
provocative image, unlike the typically more
conservative poster images of the period.
This suggestive mood is heightened by the
outline of the cat with its bulging eyes, raised
tail, and arched back.

Frank Luther Mott described *M'lle New
York,* the publication for which Powers
designed at least one poster **(cat. no. 79)**,
as "different from all other magazines except

perhaps the *Chap-Book* of Chicago. . . .
M'lle New York, a fortnightly begun August
1895 by Vance Thompson, . . . was small–qua-
tro in size, distinguished by the drawings of
T. E. Powers and Thomas Fleming, and well
printed. Its imitative French posturing, its
championship of Negro art, and its doctrine of
'autolotry' in the arts were characteristic. . . .
It published only eleven numbers in its first
series, ending with its first number for
January 1896, and then a new series of four
numbers, November 1898–January 1899."[2]

1. Peter Hastings Falk, ed., *Who Was Who in American
Art* (Boston: Sound View Press, 1985), 493.
2. Frank Luther Mott, *A History of American Magazines,
1885-1905* (Cambridge, Mass.: The Belknap Press of
Harvard University Press, 1957), 86.

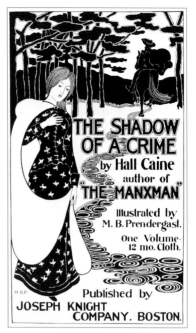

80 **On the Point**
1895
Letterpress
41.8 x 28.5 (16 1/2 x 11 1/4)
Signed lower right, inside image area: *M. B. P.*
Published by: Joseph Knight Company, Boston
Virginia Museum of Fine Arts Purchase, The Arthur and
Margaret Glasgow Fund and The Sydney and Frances
Lewis Endowment Fund, acc. no. 90.115

81 **The Shadow of a Crime**
1895
Letterpress and lithograph
38.7 x 22.2 (15 1/4 x 8 3/4)
Signed lower left: *M. B. P.*
Published by: Joseph Knight Company, Boston
Virginia Museum of Fine Arts, Gift of Dr. and Mrs. Robert
Koch, acc. no. 93.42

MAURICE BRAZIL PRENDERGAST
1859–1924

Maurice Prendergast was born in New-
foundland, but his family moved to Boston
in 1861. Leaving school at age fourteen, he
worked at a dry-goods store and learned
graphic design by designing posters for a
Boston firm.

Although a prolific painter, apparently
Prendergast produced only four posters, all
in 1895, all for Boston publishers: *Foreman
Jennie*; *On the Point*, a book by Nathan
Haskell Dole **(cat. no. 80)**; *The Shadow of a
Crime* by Hall Caine **(cat. no. 81)**; and *Round
Table Library*. He also illustrated and pro-
duced cover binding designs for three books:
The Shadow of a Crime (1895), *My Lady
Nicotine* (1896), and *Muriella* (1897).

Although these graphic illustrations can
be seen as an important part of Prendergast's
development as an artist, for the most part
they are quite different from his later, more
mature work. Here, there is undoubtedly a

self-conscious stylistic reference to the prints
and posters of Japan, with the twisting silhouettes of the figures, the stylized landscapes
and, at least in one design, the breaking of
the picture border by decorative designs.

Some of these elements continue to
appear in his later work. His watercolors of
1897, for example, "reflect the crisp edges
and compartmentalized patterning of his
poster-style graphics . . . graphic experiments
with geometric reductionism and use of Japanese compositional techniques appear. . . .
A careful analysis of these graphics reveals
an artist who was very sensitive to the latest
stylistic trends and used commercial design
to gain some professional recognition and to
realize a measure of aesthetic growth as well."[1]

Prendergast traveled to Europe, first to
England and then to Paris, where he was
influenced by the work of his French contemporaries. Upon his return to Boston, he
concentrated on his paintings and exhibited
his work more frequently.

Subsequent travels abroad, especially to
Venice, helped him to develop his mature
style by around 1912. He eventually became
a member of the artists' group known as "The
Eight" (see entry for John Sloan, page 96) and
was represented in the landmark exhibition
of Modernism, the Armory Show of 1913.

1. W. Anthony Gengarelly and Carol Derby, eds., "Maurice
Prendergast and the Applied Arts," *The Prendergasts & the
Arts & Crafts Movement: The Art of American Decoration
& Design, 1890–1920* (Williamstown, Mass.: Williams
College Museum of Art, 1989), 22.

82 **Arabella and Araminta Stories**
1895
Lithograph
68.8 x 39.3 (27 1/8 x 15 1/2)
Signed lower right in image frame: *ETHEL REED*
Published by: Copeland and Day, Boston
Printed by: Geo H. Walker & Co. Lith., Boston
Virginia Museum of Fine Arts Purchase, The Arthur and
Margaret Glasgow Fund and The Sydney and Frances
Lewis Endowment Fund, acc. no. 90.91

83 **Behind the Arras**
1895
Lithograph
71.4 x 47.0 (28 1/8 x 18 1/2)
Signed middle right on book edge: *ETHEL REED*;
    inscribed in image, lower right: *Copyright
    1895 by Lamson, Wolffe and Co., Boston*
Published by: Lamson, Wolffe and Co., Boston
Printed by: Armstrong & Co. Lithographers, Boston
Virginia Museum Purchase, The Glasgow Fund and The
Lewis Endowment Fund, acc. no. 90.84
This poster promoted the book by Bliss Carman.

ETHEL REED
1876–after 1900

Ethel Reed, a native of Newburyport, Massachusetts, was primarily self-taught, although she took drawing lessons around 1893 at Cowles School in the Boston area and studied with the miniature painter Laura Hill. By the age of eighteen, Reed had established her reputation as an illustrator.

Although she designed many posters advertising newspapers and magazines, Reed is best known for her many book posters. She also created illustrations, covers, and end papers for many of these same publications. In 1895 alone, she created sixteen posters, including one for *The Arabella and Araminta Stories* by Gertrude Smith (**cat. no. 82**), the first volume in the delightful "Yellow Haired Library" series.[1]

Her colleague, Will Bradley, wrote that "her work is . . . the result of no settled course of training, and in consequence possesses an air of freedom, almost of naiveté, that give it a distinct and individual value."[2]

Another contemporary, S. C. de Soissons,

in a rather sexist critical review, singled out Reed's work "for notice and high appreciation, not only because of its great artistic qualities, but because she does not take care of the intimate support things, she looks at the world as a gracious moving surface, infinitely shaded; she leaves success to itself, as if the world were a theatre of fairies, an adorable procession of passing impressions."[3]

A well-publicized romance and engagement to the Boston artist Philip Hale seems to have ended when she sailed alone for Europe. Reed appears to have completed her last poster in London in 1898 for Richard Le Gallienne's novel *The Quest of the Golden Girl* (**cat. no. 91**). The binding of the book itself was designed by Will Bradley. In that same year, a parody of the book, entitled *The Quest of the Gilt-Edged Girl* by Richard de Lyrienne, was published by the same publisher, John Lane, The Bodley Head, in London and New York. In Chapter 17, the narrator describes a charming girl whom he sees only

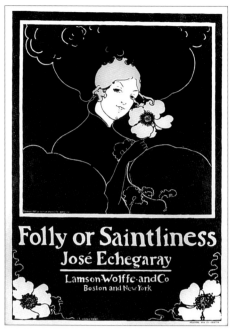

84 The Boston Sunday Herald
1895

Letterpress
48.2 x 31.7 (19 x 12 1/2)
Signed lower right inside image: *E. REED*
Published by: *The Boston Herald*
Virginia Museum of Fine Arts Purchase, The Arthur and
Margaret Glasgow Fund and The Sydney and Frances
Lewis Endowment Fund, acc. no. 90.86

85 Fairy Tales
1895

Lithograph
67.3 x 48.2 (26 1/2 x 19)
Signed lower center: *ETHEL REED*; inscribed
    lower right: *Copyright 1895 by Lamson,
    Wolffe & Co., Boston, U.S.A.*
Published by: Lamson, Wolffe & Co., Boston
Printed by: Heliotype Printing Co., Boston
Virginia Museum Purchase, The Glasgow Fund and The
Lewis Endowment Fund, acc. no. 90.90
This poster promoted the book by Mabel F. Blodgett.

86 Folly or Saintliness
1895

Letterpress, 51.3 x 38.1 (20 1/4 x 15)
Signed lower center: *ETHEL REED*; inscribed
    lower right: *HELIOTYPE PTG. CO. – BOSTON*;
    inscribed lower left of image: *Copyright 1895
    by Lamson, Wolffe & Co., Boston, U.S.A.*
Published by: Lamson, Wolffe & Co., Boston
Printed by: Heliotype Printing Co., Boston
Virginia Museum Purchase, The Glasgow Fund and The
Lewis Endowment Fund, acc. no. 90.88
This poster promoted the book by José Echegaray.

for a moment as "a diamond in a coal-scuttle;
a camellia in a waste of weeds; an Ethel Reed
poster in half an acre of Belfast litho conven-
tions; a silver salmon in a shoal of blear-eyed
cod."[4]

Ethel Reed simply disappears after the
publication of this last poster. She may have
decided to take a long rest and vacation in
Ireland, but no further record of her remains.

1. Will Bradley, "Ethel Reed, Artist," *Bradley, His Book*
(Springfield, Mass.: Wayside Press, July 1896), 74.
2. Ibid., 75.
3. S. C. de Soissons, "Ethel Reed and Her Art," *The Poster*,
vol. 1, no. 5 (November 1898): 199.
4. Richard de Lyrienne, *The Quest of the Gilt-Edged Girl*
(London and New York: John Lane, The Bodley Head,
1897), 81. We thank David R. Anderson for calling this
book and its quotation concerning Reed to our attention.

Chapter 5: Catalogue of the Collection

87 Miss Träumerei
1895
Lithograph
56.2 x 35.2 (22 1/8 x 13 7/8)
Inscribed lower right: *Copyright. 1895, by Lamson,*
Wolffe & Co., Boston; signed in print lower right:
ETHEL REED; artist's signature lower left.
Published by: Lamson, Wolffe & Co., Boston
Virginia Museum of Fine Arts Purchase, The Arthur and
Margaret Glasgow Fund and The Sydney and Frances
Lewis Endowment Fund, acc. no. 90.87
This poster promoted the book by Albert Morris Bagby.

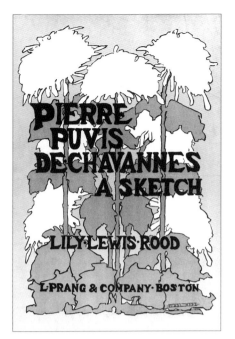

88 Pierre Puvis de Chavannes— A Sketch
1895
Lithograph
53.4 x 37.7 (21 1/4 x 14 7/8)
Signed lower right: *ETHEL REED*
Published by: Louis Prang & Co., Boston
Virginia Museum of Fine Arts Purchase, The Arthur and
Margaret Glasgow Fund and The Sydney and Frances
Lewis Endowment Fund, acc. no. 90.89
This poster promoted the book by Lily Lewis Rood.

89 A Virginia Cousin & Bar Harbor Tales
1895
Lithograph
63.2 x 43.4 (24 7/8 x 17 1/8)
Inscribed lower right: *Reed*
Published by: Lamson, Wolffe & Co., Boston
Virginia Museum of Fine Arts Purchase, The Arthur and
Margaret Glasgow Fund and The Sydney and Frances
Lewis Endowment Fund, acc. no. 90.83
This poster promoted the book by Mrs. Burton
Harrison.

ETHEL REED
Continued

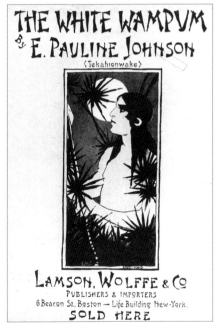

90 The White Wampum
1895
Lithograph, 57.2 x 40.6 (22 1/2 x 16)
Signed lower right inside frame: *ETHEL REED*
Published by: Lamson, Wolffe & Co., Publishers &
Importers, Boston and New York
Virginia Museum Purchase, The Glasgow Fund and The
Lewis Endowment Fund, acc. no. 90.82
This poster promoted the book by E. Pauline Johnson.
The book binding was designed by another artist.

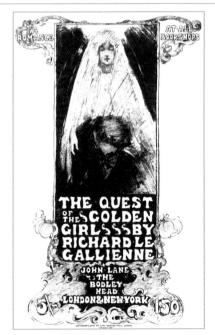

91 The Quest of the Golden Girl
1896
Lithograph, 75.2 x 48.7 (29 5/8 x 19 1/8)
Signed lower right inside image area: *ETHEL*
REED; lower center in foliate motif: *E. R.*
Published by: John Lane, The Bodley Head, London
& New York
Printed by: Waterlow & Sons, Ltd. Lithographers,
London Wall, London
Virginia Museum Purchase, The Glasgow Fund and The
Lewis Endowment Fund, acc. no. 90.85

92 **Morning Journal**
1895
Lithograph
123.4 x 152.4 (48 5/8 x 60)
Signed lower right: *L. J. R.* in heart-shaped border
Printed by: Liebler & Mass, Lithographers,
    New York
Virginia Museum of Fine Arts Purchase, The Arthur and
Margaret Glasgow Fund and The Sydney and Frances
Lewis Endowment Fund, acc. no. 90.92

LOUIS JOHN RHEAD
1857–1926

Louis John Rhead came from an English family of artists: his father was an artist at the Wedgwood Pottery factory and his two brothers, Frederick Alfred Rhead and George Woolliscroft Rhead, were also artists and craftsmen. Born in Etruria, Staffordshire, England, Louis Rhead studied at the South Kensington Art School and later in Paris. During this time he designed book jackets and posters for *Cassell's Magazine* before coming to New York, where he worked as an illustrator for D. Appleton Company. Although he served as Appleton's art director, he also contributed freelance work to other companies.

In 1891 he returned to London and then Paris, where he became acquainted with the work of Eugène Grasset. Much has been written about Grasset's influence on Rhead, particularly in his use of planes of color and broad outlines and his emphasis on close-ups of figures. David Kiehl feels that the relationship between the two artists was one of "parallel development."[1]

Rhead's posters, especially those done for the printing firm of Louis Prang, were favorites among collectors and the general public alike. In the mid 1890s, around 20,000 copies of his posters were printed.[2] His poster advertising *Prang's Easter Publications* (**cat. no. 94**) is considered "the most valuable Prang poster today."[3]

The hand-written inscription on the Virginia Museum's copy of Rhead's poster *Read the Sun* (**cat. no. 93**) points up the desire of both fellow artists and collectors to obtain copies of Rhead's posters as quickly as they were printed.

Before the turn of the century Louis Rhead designed as many as one hundred

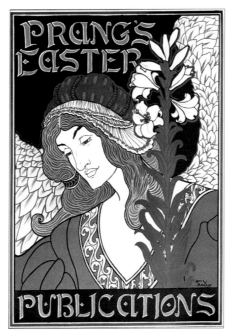

93 **Read the Sun**
1895
Lithograph, 118.7 x 71.1 (46 3/4 x 28)
Signed lower left: *L. J. R.* in heart shape; inscribed
lower right in ink: *To Wilbur M. Stone / Hartford*
Conn. / with regards / Louis J. Rhead / This
copy and one I am / sending to Bolton are /
the 2 first allowed to leave the "sun" office
Published by: New York Sun
Virginia Museum Purchase, The Glasgow Fund and The
Lewis Endowment Fund, acc. no. 90.96

94 **Prang's Easter Publications**
1895
Lithograph
60.6 x 43.2 (23 7.8 x 17)
Signed lower right, in image area: *Louis/Rhead*
Published by: Louis Prang & Co., Boston
Virginia Museum of Fine Arts Purchase, The Arthur and
Margaret Glasgow Fund and The Sydney and Frances
Lewis Endowment Fund, acc. no. 90.98

95 **L. Prang & Co.'s Holiday**
Publications, 1895
Lithograph
55.8 x 41.2 (22 x 16 1/4)
Signed lower right, in image area: *L. J./RHEAD*
Published by: Louis Prang & Co., Boston
Virginia Museum of Fine Arts Purchase, The Arthur and
Margaret Glasgow Fund and The Sydney and Frances
Lewis Endowment Fund, acc. no. 90.97

LOUIS JOHN RHEAD
Continued

posters for periodicals, books, and newspapers, and for products such as Lundborg
perfumes, Pearline washing powders and
cleansers, and Packer's soap.[4]

The essence of Rhead's posters—and a
possible reason for their popularity—was
captured in a statement by his contemporary
Gleeson White: "The secret of the poster is
not one to be hidden, but to be loudly proclaimed. . . . Audacity and arrogance befit a
placard, and if the man in the street jeers at
blue haired maidens, or emerald green skies,
do not assume too hastily that the artist who
employs them has blundered. . . . The diffi-
culty is to be eccentric and yet to keep
within the bounds of good taste."[5]

1. David W. Kiehl, *American Art Posters of the 1890s in
The Metropolitan Museum of Art, including the Leonard
A. Lauder Collection* (New York: The Metropolitan Museum
of Art; distributed by Harry N. Abrams, 1987), 191.
2. Ruth Malhotra and Christina Thon, *Das frühe Plakat
in Europa und den USA*, vol. 1: *Grossbritannien und
Vereinigte Staaten von Nordamerika* (Berlin: Gebr. Mann,
1973), ii–iv.
3. Katharine Morrison McClinton, *The Chromolithographs of Louis Prang* (New York: Clarkson N. Potter,
1973), 22.
4. Peter Hastings Falk, ed., *Who Was Who in American
Art* (Boston: Sound View Press, 1985), 514.
5. Gleeson White, "The Posters of Louis Rhead," *The
Studio*, vol. 8, no. 41 (August 1896): 19.

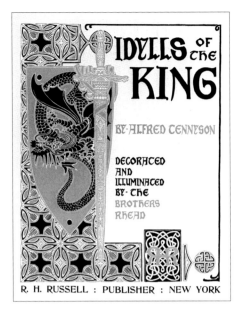

96 **Meadow-Grass**
1895
Lithograph
43.2 x 25.4 (17 x 10)
Signed lower right, in letters stacked vertically:
RHEAD
Published by: Copeland and Day, Boston
Printed by: Geo. H. Walker & Co. Lith., Boston
Virginia Museum Purchase, The Glasgow Fund and The
Lewis Endowment Fund, acc. no. 90.93
This same design was used on the book by Alice Brown.

97 **The Pocket Magazine**
1896
Lithograph (aluminography)
126.3 x 78.7 (49 3/4 x 31)
Signed center left: *LJR* in heart shape
Printed by: The Ellery Howard Co., New York
Virginia Museum of Fine Arts Purchase, The Arthur and
Margaret Glasgow Fund and The Sydney and Frances
Lewis Endowment Fund, acc. no. 90.94

98 **Idylls of the King**
1896
Letterpress
36.5 x 31.7 (14 1/2 x 31.7)
Unsigned
Published by: R. H. Russell, Publisher, New York
Virginia Museum of Fine Arts Purchase, The Arthur and
Margaret Glasgow Fund and The Sydney and Frances
Lewis Endowment Fund, acc. no. 90.95

THE BROTHERS RHEAD
Louis John Rhead (1857-1926)
George Woolliscroft Rhead (1855-1920)

This poster, the result of a collaboration
between two of the Rhead brothers, Louis
and George, was designed to promote the
book by the noted British author Alfred,
Lord Tennyson.

99 **International October**
1896
Letterpress
43.5 x 23.8 (17 1/8 x 9 3/8)
Signed lower right: *Frederick Richardson*
Virginia Museum of Fine Arts, Gift of Dr. and Mrs. Robert
Koch, acc. no. 93.44

FREDERICK RICHARDSON
1862–1937

Painter, illustrator, and publisher Frederick Richardson was born in Chicago and studied both at the St. Louis School of Fine Arts and in Paris. His paintings were shown at the Paris Salon of 1889. He contributed illustrations to *The Chicago Daily News* and designed posters for the magazines *International* (**cat. no. 99**) and *St. Nicholas*.

In 1900 Richardson founded his own magazine, *International Monthly*, in Burlington, Vermont, where he was a university professor.[1] The magazine was "designed for the interchange of ideas among the world's thinkers" without being too technical for the average reader.[2] Its twelve departments— history, philosophy, psychology, sociology, religion, fine arts, industrial art, physics, biology, medicine and hygiene, geology, and geography—were managed by an advisory board that included well-known experts in each field who also served as contributors. The journal became the *International*

Quarterly in December 1902, when the price was raised from three to five dollars for a subscription, but "it failed to make a permanent place for itself"[3] and folded after five-and-a-half years of publication.

From 1905 until his death in New York City on January 14, 1937, Richardson worked primarily as a book illustrator. Among his numerous projects were *Queen Zixi of IX*, by L. Frank Baum, 1905; *Mother Goose*, edited by Eulalie Osgood Grover, 1915; and *Little Folk, the Story of an Indian Boy*, by Katherine Louise Keelor, 1917.[4]

The style of the poster illustrated here, with its complex integration of design and typography, owes a debt to Will Bradley.

1. Frank Luther Mott, *A History of American Magazines, 1885–1905* (Cambridge, Mass.: The Belknap Press of Harvard University Press, 1957), 225.
2. Ibid.
3. Ibid.
4. Theodore Bolton, *American Book Illustrators: Bibliographic Check List of 123 Artists* (New York: R. R. Bowker Company, 1938), 168-69.

100 **The Century for September**
1896
Lithograph
53.3 x 36.8 (21 x 14 1/2)
Signed lower left: *H. M. Rosenberg*; inscribed:
   COPYRIGHT, 1896 BY THE CENTURY CO.;
   inscribed lower right: *G. H. BUEK & CO.,*
   LITHOGRAPHERS, N.Y.
Published by: The Century Company, New York
Printed by: G. H. Buek & Co., New York
Virginia Museum Purchase, The Glasgow Fund and The
Lewis Endowment Fund, acc. no. 90.102

HENRY MORTIKAR ROSENBERG
1858–1947

Henry Mortikar Rosenberg was another artist of this period who was greatly influenced by the painter and etcher Frank Duveneck. According to Rosenberg biographers Robert Stacey and Liz Wylie, Rosenberg was one of Duveneck's "boys," a group of his students who followed the master to Munich, Paris, Florence, and then to Venice.[1] There they met the American artist James McNeill Whistler, who became the center of the entourage and whose work, especially as an etcher, had great influence on Rosenberg.

Stacey and Wylie have categorized Rosenberg's work into four main groups: landscapes and seascapes in oils and watercolors; portraits and decorative figure compositions in oils, chalks, and pastels; fantasy pieces, *jeux-d'esprit*, and caricatures in various media; and, "his first love," etching.[2]

His only known poster (**cat. no. 100**), received an honorable mention in *The Century* magazine's midsummer contest of 1896. This poster lacks the graphic immediacy of works by such artists as Penfield, Rhead, or Bradley; rather it is more of a delicate drawing.

In a 1906 lecture, Rosenberg presented his views about the philosophy of art and art education. He argued that "art is . . . one of the deepest and most far reaching influences on a community. The Art Idea lies more or less latent in all, needing only environment and training to forward it to its utmost capacity for usefulness. . . . "[3]

1. Robert Stacey and Liz Wylie, *Eighty/Twenty: 100 Years of the Nova Scotia College of Art and Design* (Nova Scotia, Canada: Art Gallery of Nova Scotia, 1988), 39.
2. Ibid., 41.
3. Ibid., 42.

101 **Quo Vadis**
1897
Lithograph
72.7 X 50.1 (28 5/8 X 19 3/4)
Signed across bottom: *J. A. SCHWEINFURTH FECIT,*
BOSTON, MDCCCXCVII
Published by: Little, Brown & Co., Boston
Printed by: Geo. H. Walker & Co. Lith., Boston
Virginia Museum of Fine Arts Purchase, The Arthur and
Margaret Glasgow Fund and The Sydney and Frances
Lewis Endowment Fund, acc. no. 90.103

JULIUS A. SCHWEINFURTH
1858-1931

After studying in Paris, Julius Schweinfurth practiced architecture in Boston. The Boston City Directories from 1887 and 1930 indicate that he moved both his office and his home three times during this period.[1] Although the catalogue of an 1895 exhibition notes that Mrs. Schweinfurth lent "a number" of posters to the exhibition, only two by Schweinfurth are known. One of these was for the Boston Festival Orchestra, and the other advertised the novel *Quo Vadis,* a book by Henry K. Sienkiewicz **(cat. no. 101)**.[2]

As an architect, Schweinfurth received important commissions, including one for the New England College of Optometry on Beacon Street in Boston. One can only speculate why a successful, traditionally trained architect would be commissioned to design posters for a major publishing house such as Little, Brown & Co. The fact that he was not trained as a graphic designer, but as an architect, might account for the seeming awkwardness in the figure and the lack of cohesion between the typography, the figure in the foreground, and the background scene.

1. Information contained in a letter to the author dated July 17, 1992, from Bridget Knightly, Library Assistant, The Bostonian Society.
2. David W. Kiehl, *American Art Posters of the 1890s in The Metropolitan Museum of Art, including the Leonard A. Lauder Collection* (New York: The Metropolitan Museum of Art; distributed by Harry N. Abrams, 1987), 192.

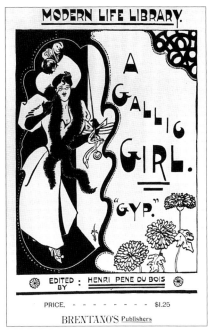

102 **A Gallic Girl**
ca. 1895
Letterpress
56.5 x 37.4 (22 1/4 x 14 3/4)
Unsigned
Published by: Brentano's, New York
Virginia Museum of Fine Arts Purchase, The Arthur and
Margaret Glasgow Fund and The Sydney and Frances
Lewis Endowment Fund, acc. no. 90.104

103 **The New York Sunday World**
1895
Letterpress
45.7 x 30.5 (18 x 12)
Signed lower center: *Scotson-Clark*
Published by: The New York World, New York
Virginia Museum of Fine Arts, Gift of Dr. and Mrs. Robert
Koch, acc. no. 93.45

GEORGE FREDERICK SCOTSON-CLARK
1873–?

English-born Scotson-Clark lived in Brighton until 1891, when he came to America. In New York he worked for various theaters designing stage sets, costumes, and posters.

Scotson-Clark is credited with creating the first American newspaper poster for the *New York Recorder* in 1895.[1] In an article he mentioned that the same drawing, "done in supposedly Beardsleyesque style," appeared two weeks later, on June 6, 1895, in *The Chicago Times Herald*.[2] He designed other posters for New York newspapers and magazines including *The New York World* (**see cat. no. 103**).

In 1897 Scotson-Clark returned to England. In *The Poster* of November 1900, he wrote a brief article entitled "The Black Spot in America," in which he discussed the use of the "black spot" or solid black mass as an element of composition and its "invasion" in the graphic arts of the United States, through the work of the English artist (and former classmate) Aubrey Beardsley.[3] This characteristic "black spot" design is apparent in his poster for *A Gallic Girl,* a book edited by Henri Pène du Bois. Many graphic artists in this country utilized variations of Beardsley's compositional devices, but eluded the "immorality" associated with the work of the Englishman. In his closing remarks, Scotson-Clark wrote:

> It is regrettable, but nevertheless a fact, that Beardsley unwittingly did a lot of harm. His style was easy to copy, and a great many men who had little or no knowledge of drawing were thus enabled by imitating his work to make a living, and therefore men who would otherwise have been earning an honest wage at mud-shovelling or mending the roads, were allowed to plunge into a 'vortex of artistry,' to cheat themselves into the belief that they were artists, and to bamboozle the man blessed with more money than taste out of his dollars."[4]

1. Victor Margolin, *American Poster Renaissance* (New York: Watson-Guptill, 1975), 217.
2. George Frederick Scotson-Clark, "The Black Spot in America," *The Poster* (November 1900): 84–87.
3. Ibid.
4. Ibid.

104 **The Echo**
1895
Letterpress
47.6 x 21.0 (18 3/4 x 8 1/4)
Signed lower right: *John/Sloan*
Printed by: The Chicago Photo Engravers Co.,
 Chicago
Virginia Museum of Fine Arts Purchase, The Arthur and
Margaret Glasgow Fund and The Sydney and Frances
Lewis Endowment Fund, acc. no. 90.105

JOHN SLOAN
1871–1951

In 1908 a small group of American painters rebelled against the National Academy of Design and its system of juried exhibitions and instead exhibited their work together at the Macbeth Gallery in New York. The group, formed by Robert Henri, initially included John Sloan and three other Realists working in New York—George Luks, William Glackens, and Everett Shinn—and later included the Impressionist Ernest Lawson, the Romantic painter Arthur B. Davies, and the Boston Neo-Impressionist Maurice Prendergast **(see cat. nos. 80, 81,** p. 85).[1] They became known as "The Eight" or, because of their urban subject matter, "The Ashcan School."

Several members of this new group had studied and worked together, many of them having begun as illustrators. John Sloan, one of the leading artists in this group, worked as an illustrator for *The Philadelphia Inquirer* and other local papers in the last part of the nineteenth century.

His illustrations, such as his 1895 design for *The Echo*, show the influence of Japanese stylistic imagery as well as that of his French and English contemporaries. The bold outlines of the figure in *The Echo* resemble those of a woodcut, although the technique of printing was letterpress. This stylistic trait shows Sloan's concern for graphic design, which continued in his paintings and particularly in his prints.

A prolific artist, Sloan undoubtedly created a great number of poster and advertisement designs, but the exact number has not been determined.[2]

1. See: *Oxford Companion to Twentieth-Century Art*, ed. Harold Osborne, (Oxford: Oxford Univ. Press, 1981), 173.
2. David W. Kiehl, *American Art Posters of the 1890s in The Metropolitan Museum of Art, including the Leonard A. Lauder Collection* (New York: Metropolitan Museum of Art; distributed by Harry N. Abrams, 1987), 192.

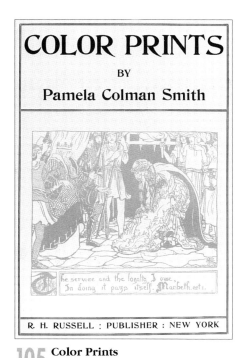

COLOR PRINTS

BY

Pamela Colman Smith

R. H. RUSSELL : PUBLISHER : NEW YORK

105 **Color Prints**
1898
Letterpress
46.1 x 32.0 (18 1/8 x 12 5/8)
Signed lower right in image area: artist's monogram;
    inscribed: *Copyrighted by W. B. Macbeth,
    NY/1898*
Published by: R. H. Russell, Publisher, New York
Virginia Museum of Fine Arts Purchase, The Arthur and
Margaret Glasgow Fund and The Sydney and Frances
Lewis Endowment Fund, acc. no. 90.100

PAMELA COLMAN SMITH
1877/78–ca.1950

The exact date of Pamela Colman Smith's birth is unknown, but her biographer, Melinda Boyd Parsons, believes that she was born in either 1877 or 1878. Although the United States was her birthplace, she lived in England until the age of 10 and then in New York City from 1893 to 1899.[1]

During this period of her life in New York, she enrolled at the Pratt Institute, where she studied under Arthur Wesley Dow, the noted teacher, painter, and illustrator. Her life goals, which seem to have developed at this time, were teaching and illustration. Many of her finest illustrations, such as the Virginia Museum's poster for her own book of prints (**cat. no. 105**), date from this period. Upon graduation she was successful in selling her illustrations through the Macbeth Gallery and to various periodicals and newspapers. In addition, she published a number of books of both her writings and illustrations.

Smith moved back to England in 1899 and continued her prolific career there. Although she established her permanent residence in England, she occasionally returned to the United States, and she also exhibited her drawings at Alfred Stieglitz's gallery *291* on Fifth Avenue in New York. Smith was the first nonphotographic artist to show at this avant-garde gallery. Although some photographer-artists objected to his showing Smith's work, Stieglitz defended it for its honesty and self-expression. Her drawing "marked not a departure from the intentions of the Photo-Secession, but a welcome opportunity of their manifesting. The Secession is neither the servant nor the product of a medium. It is . . . the Spirit of the lamp of honesty . . . and when these pictures of Miss Smith's, conceived in this spirit and no others, came to us . . . we but tended the lamp in tendering them hospitality."[2]

1. For full information on Smith's biography see Melinda Boyd Parsons, *To All Believers—The Art of Pamela Colman Smith* (Wilmington: Delaware Art Museum, 1975).
2. Ibid, unpaginated.

106 **July 1895 Outing**
1895
Letterpress and photomechanical halftone
55.6 x 35.9 (21 7/8 x 14 1/8)
Signed right center in vertically stacked letters:
 H · S · WATSON · 95
Published by: J. H. Worman, New York
Virginia Museum of Fine Arts, Gift of Dr. and Mrs. Robert
Koch, acc. no. 93.46

107 **Recreation, August**
1896
Letterpress
41.9 x 34.8 (16 1/2 x 13 3/4)
Signed lower left: *HY · S · WATSON*; inscribed lower
 left: *PRESS OF E. SCOTT CO., 148 WEST 23D
 STREET, N.Y.*
Printed by: E. Scott Co., New York
Virginia Museum of Fine Arts Purchase, The Arthur and
Margaret Glasgow Fund and The Sydney and Frances
Lewis Endowment Fund, acc. no. 90.116

HENRY SUMNER WATSON
1868-1933

Born in Bordentown, New Jersey, Henry S. Watson studied at the Pennsylvania Academy of the Fine Arts with Thomas Eakins and at the Académie Julian in Paris. After returning to America, Watson worked as an illustrator specializing in hunting and fishing scenes. *Truth, Outing, Recreation* (**cat. no. 107**), and *Bachelor of Arts* published his work. From 1895 to 1897 Watson designed around forty posters,[1] and he eventually became editor of *Field and Stream*.[2]

Outing, one of the magazines for which Watson designed illustrations (**cat. no. 106**), was founded in Albany, New York, by William Bailey Howland in May 1882. Priced at twenty cents, it was a comparatively expensive magazine appealing to those interested in outdoor sports such as hunting, fishing, bicycling, and yachting.[3]

It is interesting to compare the two Watson posters in this catalogue, which were done within a year of one another. The 1895 *Outing* poster is very subtle in its use of the relatively new technology of photomechanical halftone printing. The artist has superimposed the photograph of a sailboat upon a delicately drawn image that hints at the presence of a man and a woman carrying a parasol. They are surrounded by tendrils of flowers in the Art Nouveau manner. The bold lettering of the date of issue and the title are a marked contrast.

The design for *Recreation*, done a year later, has a more cartoonlike appearance and is typical of Watson's humorous approach to his illustrations, which usually featured an outdoorsman and his faithful dachshund. In this case, the dog seems to be worried about his master's possible drowning.

1. David W. Kiehl, *American Art Posters of the 1890s in The Metropolitan Museum of Art, including the Leonard A. Lauder Collection* (New York: The Metropolitan Museum of Art; distributed by Harry N. Abrams, Inc.), 192.
2. Peter Hastings Falk, ed., *Who Was Who in American Art* (Boston: Sound View Press, 1985), 662.
3. Frank Luther Mott, *A History of American Magazines, 1885-1905* (Cambridge, Mass.: The Belknap Press of Harvard University Press, 1957), 633.

108 **Opera Stories**
1896
Lithograph
71.7 x 35.5 (28 1/4 x 14)
Signed lower left: *Irene/Weir* in box
Published by: H. L. Mason, Boston
Printed by: W. B. Jones Lithographer, Boston
Virginia Museum of Fine Arts Purchase, The Arthur and
Margaret Glasgow Fund and The Sydney and Frances
Lewis Endowment Fund, acc no. 90.106

IRENE WEIR
1862–1944

Irene Weir was the granddaughter of artist Robert Walter Weir (whose biography she wrote in 1947), the daughter of his eldest son Walter, and the niece of artists J. Alden Weir and John Ferguson Weir. As she notes in the foreword of her book about her grandfather, "Art as a profession came naturally to her, and to four Weir cousins, bringing the inheritance of the Weir facility in art to the present day, one hundred and forty-one years of a family talent."[1]

Weir was born in St. Louis and, according to Boston City Directories, lived in Boston from 1899 to 1902.[2] She received her B.F.A. from Yale University, where she studied with her uncle J. Alden Weir, John Henry Twachtman, and Joseph Pennell. She also studied abroad at the Colarossi School and in 1923 received a diploma from the Ecole des Beaux-Arts Americain at Fountainbleau.

In addition to working as a printmaker and poster illustrator, Weir painted portraits and murals. Her grandfather, Robert W. Weir, founded the art department of the Military Academy at West Point, New York, and Weir herself was founder of the School of Design and Liberal Arts in New York City. She wrote a number of books dealing with various art-historical subjects and, at the time of her death, was working on the manuscript for her book, *Three Weirs, Artists*.

1. Irene Weir, *Robert W. Weir, Artist* (New York: New York House of Field, Doubleday, 1947), iii.
2. Information courtesy of The Bostonian Society, Boston, Massachusetts.

109 **Boston Park Guide**
1895
Lithograph
48.8 x 30.5 (19 1/4 x 12)
Signed lower left: *Chas H. Woodbury*
Published by: Sylvester Baxter
Virginia Museum of Fine Arts Purchase, The Arthur and
Margaret Glasgow Fund and The Sydney and Frances
Lewis Endowment Fund, acc. no. 90.108

*This poster promoted a guidebook to Boston by
Sylvester Baxter.*

110 **The July Century**
1895
Letterpress and lithograph
48.2 x 29.8 (19 x 11 3/4)
Signed lower left: *Chas H. Woodbury*
Published by: The Century Company, New York
Virginia Museum of Fine Arts Purchase, The Arthur and
Margaret Glasgow Fund and The Sydney and Frances
Lewis Endowment Fund, acc. no. 90.107

111 **The May Century**
1897
Lithograph
52.7 x 30.5 (20 3/4 x 12)
Signed lower left: *CHW*
Published by: The Century Company, New York
Virginia Museum of Fine Arts Purchase, The Arthur and
Margaret Glasgow Fund and The Sydney and Frances
Lewis Endowment Fund, acc. no. 90.117

CHARLES HERBERT WOODBURY
1864–1940

Charles H. Woodbury was born in Lynn,
Massachusetts. After graduating from the
Massachusetts Institute of Technology, he
studied in Paris at the Académie Julian and
then evidently also spent some time studying
in Holland. Noted for his seascapes, Woodbury
worked as a successful painter in Boston.

Woodbury's poster designs are known for
their sparsity of detail, with an emphasis on
flat planes of color, bold outlines, and distinc-
tive integration of typography and subject
matter. Much of this was undoubtedly due to
the influence he received in France as well
as to his interest in the stylistic treatments
found in Japanese prints. This is particularly
evident in his design for *The July Century*,
(cat. no. 110), the subject of which is
American summer festivals.[1]

Of his work Woodbury once said: "My
general interest in line is for its suggestive
value, as it conveys the thought of force of
motion. . . . It is as abstract as a word and
stands for the sensation as a word does for
an object."[2]

Woodbury wrote several books, including
Painting and the Personal Equation (1922)
and *The Art of Seeing* (1925). He was a member of numerous artistic societies, including
the National Academy of Design.

1. David W. Kiehl, *American Art Posters of the 1890s in
The Metropolitan Museum of Art, including the Leonard
A. Lauder Collection* (New York: The Metropolitan Museum
of Art; distributed by Harry N. Abrams, 1987), 182.
2. Una E. Johnson, *American Prints and Printmakers*
(Garden City, New York: Doubleday & Co., 1980), 29.

Select Bibliography

Historic Sources

Alexandre, Arsène, H. C. Bunner, August Jaccaci, and M. H. Spielmann. *The Modern Poster.* New York: Charles Scribner's Sons, 1895.

Bradley, Will H. "Edward Penfield, Artist." *Bradley, His Book,* vol. 1, no. 1 (May 1896).

———. *Will Bradley: His Chap-Book.* New York: The Typophiles, 1955.

Bragdon, Claude Fayette. *Poster Lore,* book 1, part 3 (April 1896).

———. "American Posters, Past and Present." *Scribner's Magazine* 18 (October 1895).

Clemens, Will M. *The Poster,* vol. 1, no. 2 (February 1896).

Crane, Walter. *Decorative Illustration.* London and New York: George Bell, 1896.

Cunningham, Roger. "Cui Bono?" *Poster Lore,* book 1, part 4 (July 1896).

De Soissons, S. C. "Ethel Reed and Her Art." *The Poster* (November 1898).

E. G. G. "Sketches and Impressions of an American Printer." *The American Printer* (January 20, 1924): 42-46.

Faxon, Frederick Winthrop. *Ephemeral Bibelots: A Bibliography of Modern Chap-Books and Their Imitators.* Boston: The Boston Book Company, 1903.

Hartmann, Sadakichi. *A History of American Art* 2. Boston: L. C. Page & Company, 1902.

Hiatt, Charles. *Picture Posters.* London: George Bell and Sons, 1895.

———. "The Collecting of Posters. A New Field for Connoisseurs." *The Studio,* vol. 1, no. 2 (May 1893): 61-62.

Konody, P. G. *The Art of Walter Crane.* London: George Bell & Sons, 1902.

Les affiches etrangères illustrées. Paris: G. Boudet, 1897.

Les maîtres de l'affiche. Paris: Imprimerie Chaix, 1896-99.

Lincoln, George. "Machine Composition Notes and Queries." *The Inland Printer* (February 1899).

Maindron, Ernest. "Les affiches illustrées." *Gazette des Beaux-Arts* 30 (1884).

———. *Les affiches illustrées.* Paris: H. Launette, 1886.

———. *Les affiches illustrées, 1886-1895.* Paris, 1896.

Penfield, Edward. *Posters in Miniature.* New York: R. H. Russell and Son, 1896.

Price, Charles Matlack. *Poster Design: A Critical Study of the Development of the Poster in Continental Europe, England, and America,* new and enlarged edition. New York: George W. Bricka, 1913.

Singleton, Frederic Thoreau. "Notes." *Poster Lore,* book 1, part 4 (July 1896): 121.

Steevens, George W. *The Land of the Dollar.* New York: publisher unknown, 1897.

Talmeyer, Maurice. "The Age of the Poster." *The Chautauquan* 24 (January 1897).

Modern Sources

Thompson, John Smith. *The Mechanism of the Linotype*. Chicago: The Inland Printer, 1902.

——. *History of Composing Machines*. Chicago: The Inland Printer, 1904.

Tuckerman, Henry T. *Book of the Artists: American Artist Life*. New York: G.P. Putnam's Sons, 1867.

"Will Bradley, Artist," *Chicago Sunday Tribune*, December 30, 1894.

Baker, Elizabeth Faulkner. *Printers and Technology*. Westport, Conn.: Greenwood Press, 1957.

Black, Mary C. *American Advertising Posters of the Nineteenth Century*. New York: Dover Publications, 1976.

Breitenbach, Edgar. "A Brief History." *The American Poster*. New York: American Federation of Arts, 1967.

——. "The Poster Craze." *American Heritage*, vol. 13, no. 2 (February 1962).

Eckman, James. *The Heritage of the Printer*. Philadelphia: North American Publishing Company, 1965.

Goddu, Joseph. *American Art Posters of the 1890s*. New York: Hirschl & Adler Galleries, 1990.

Howells, William Dean. *Criticism and Fiction*. New York, 1891; reprint, New York: New York University Press, 1959.

Johnson, Diane Chalmers. *American Art Nouveau*. New York: Harry N. Abrams, 1979.

Keay, Carolyn. *American Posters of the Turn of the Century*. New York: St. Martin's Press, 1975.

Kiehl, David W. *American Art Posters of the 1890s in The Metropolitan Museum of Art, including the Leonard A. Lauder Collection*. New York: The Metropolitan Museum of Art; distributed by Harry N. Abrams, New York, 1987.

Koch, Robert. "Artistic Books, Periodicals and Posters of the 'Gay Nineties'." *The Art Quarterly*, vol. 25, no. 4 (Winter 1962).

——. "The Poster Movement and 'Art Nouveau'." *Gazette des Beaux-Arts* 50 (1957).

——. "Will Bradley." *Art in America* 3 (1962).

Lambourne, Lionel. "The Poster and the Popular Arts of the 1890s." *High Art and Low Life: The Studio and the Fin de Siècle*, vol. 201, no. 1022-23 (1993).

Margolin, Victor. *American Poster Renaissance*. New York: Watson-Guptill, 1975.

Marzio, Peter C. *The Democratic Art: Pictures for a 19th-Century America*. Boston: David R. Godine, 1979.

Meech, Julia, and Gabriel Weisberg. *Japonisme Comes to America*. New York: Harry N. Abrams, 1990.

Meggs, Philip B. *A History of Graphic Design*, 2nd ed. New York: Van Nostrand Reinhold, 1992.

Morse, Peter. "The American Poster Period: 1893-1897." *Auction Magazine* 3 (October 1969).

Mott, Frank Luther. "Magazine Revolution and Popular Ideas." *American Antiquarian Society Proceedings* 64 (April 1954).

Pierce, Sally, and Catharine Slautterback. *Boston Lithography: 1825-1880*. Boston: The Boston Athenaeum, 1991.

Rennert, Jack. *Poster Potpourri*. New York: Poster Auctions International, 1988.

Wichmann, Siegfried. *Japonisme: The Japanese Influence on Western Art in the 19th and 20th Century*. New York: Harmony Books, 1981.

Index

About the Authors

Frederick R. Brandt, Curator of 20th-Century Art at the Virginia Museum of Fine Arts, is a scholar of European and American painting, graphics, sculpture, and decorative arts of the late 19th through the 20th century.

In addition to *Designed to Sell,* Brandt has authored many works in his field, including catalogues for the Virginia Museum on *Art Nouveau* (1971), *Late 20th-Century Art, Late 19th-Early 20th Century Decorative Arts* (both 1985), and *German-Expressionist Art* (1987), as well as articles for *The Magazine Antiques* and *Apollo.*

Robert Koch, Professor Emeritus, Southern Connecticut State University, is considered one of the nation's foremost authorities on turn-of-the-century decorative arts.

His books and articles on Art Nouveau, Tiffany glass, and other European and American arts and crafts include *Louis Comfort Tiffany, Rebel in Glass* (Crown, 1964), *Louis C. Tiffany's Art Glass* (Crown, 1977), and articles on "Elbert Hubbard's Roycrofters as Artist-Craftsmen," for *Winterthur Portfolio* (1967) and "Will Bradley" for *Art in America* (1967).

Philip B. Meggs, author of the essential *History of Graphic Design* (Van Nostrand Reinhold, 1983, 1993; Spanish ed. 1993) and *Typographic Design: Form and Communication* (VNR, 1985, 1993), is a Professor in the Department of Communication Arts & Design at Virginia Commonwealth University, Richmond.

He has served as a contributing editor to *Print* magazine, was a juror for the *Washington Illustrators Club* in 1989 and the *Communication Arts Design Annual* in 1991, and is a member of the American Institute of Graphic Arts.

About the Book

Produced by the Office of Publications, Virginia Museum of Fine Arts, 2800 Grove Avenue, Richmond, Virginia 23221-2466 USA

Edited by Monica S. Rumsey with editorial assistance from Rosalie A. West and Anne Lew

Editorial keyboarding by Best Secretarial Services, Richmond, Virginia

Graphic design and production by Jean Kane

Poster photography, except where noted, is by Ron Jennings, Ann Hutchison, and Grace Wen Hwa Ts'ao. Photographic printing by Denise Lewis.

The text was set on the Macintosh using QuarkXPress in a digitized version of Garamond, a rendering of the type first cut by Claude Garamond (c. 1480–1561).

Printed on Warren's Lustro Dull 80# Text by Sterling Printers, Inc., Richmond, Virginia